How to Listen to God

A Guide for Successful Living Through the Practice of Two-way Prayer

How to Listen to God

A Guide for Successful Living Through the Practice of Two-way Prayer

Wally Paton

Faith With Works Publishing Company
Tucson, AZ

Published by Faith With Works Publishing Company
P.O. Box 91648, Tucson, AZ 85752-1648
tel.: (520) 297-9348   fax.: (520) 297-7230
http://www.faithwithworks.com http://www.aabacktobasics.org

Please direct all inquiries about the *Converting Barriers to Bridges* program of recovery, renewal and regeneration (Chapters 5–11) to Faith With Works Publishing Company.

First Printing: December 2000

Library of Congress Cataloging-in-Publication Data

Paton, Wally
    How to Listen to God: a guide for successful living through the practice of two-way prayer
    p.   cm.
    Includes bibliographical references and appendices.
    Preassigned LCCN: 00-093289
    ISBN: 0-9657720-4-7
    1. James Houck–Biography. 2. Oxford Group. 3. Prayer and Meditation–spirituality. 4. Twelve Step Movement
    5. Substance abuse–recovery. I. Title.

Printed in the United States of America
10 9 8 7 6 5 4 3 2

Dedication

This book is dedicated to my mentor, spiritual advisor and sharing partner, James Houck. James attended Oxford Group meetings from 1935-1937 with Bill Wilson, the New York City co-founder of the Twelve Step Movement. James obtained a copy of *How to Listen to God* from John Batterson in the late 1930's and has incorporated the principles of this four-page pamphlet into his life-changing work for the past sixty-five years.

This book is also dedicated to John Batterson, the author of the *How to Listen to God* pamphlet that has done much to change the world by bringing people closer to God through the practice of two-way prayer. John was an Oxford Group pioneer who attended meetings and house parties in the 1930's with Dr. Bob and Anne Smith. Dr. Bob is the Akron, Ohio co-founder of the Twelve Step Movement.

Contents

Acknowledgments

I am grateful for the encouragement and support I have received during the three years it has taken me to write this tribute to James Houck, one of America's greatest life-changers. James is living proof that the Four Step program of the 1930's worked then and is continuing to work today.

I am indebted to Bonnie and Ozzie Lepper, the proprietors of the Wilson House, for providing me the opportunity to present the *Back to Basics* and *Converting Barriers to Bridges* programs at weekend spiritual retreats during the past four years. Much of the material for this book came directly from those very successful, life-saving seminars.

I am extending a special thanks to Sue Smith Windows, Dr. Bob and Anne Smith's daughter for making her mom and dad's archival materials available. This collection provided me with a great deal of insight into the original Four Step program that changed so many lives in the 1930's.

I also wish to thank those who helped critique, edit and pray over this book. Some of them are Neil Britner, Jeffrey Duck, John and Susan Hutzler, and Bill Lash. In addition, Mickie Jones assisted with the production of the final manuscript and Margaret Allen, along with Susan Slenk, did much of the typing of the Oxford Group source material.

How to Listen to God

A Guide for Successful Living
Through the Practice of
Two-way Prayer

1

The Journey Begins

There was a period of time when I did not know how to listen to God. I only vaguely remember those dark days of hopelessness and despair, even though they accounted for nearly fifty years of my life. Then, I was transformed–shown how to walk in the sunlight of the spirit. I have James Houck to thank for this conversion experience.

James is ninety-four years old and has been listening to God for more than sixty-five of those years. He discovered the miracle of two-way prayer in the Oxford Group, an evangelical, spiritual movement that was prominent during the 1930's. He met the Group on December 12, 1934–one day after Bill Wilson, the New York City co-founder of the Twelve Step Movement. James attended meetings with Bill from 1935-1937.

By taking the Oxford Group Four Steps of Surrender, Sharing, Restitution and Guidance, James found a new way of living. These were the same steps taken by Bill Wilson, Dr. Bob Smith and the others who helped write the "Big Book" in 1939.

I talked with James on the telephone in February 1996. I met him in person three weeks later. By following his suggestions and the Group plan of action, I was released from the shackles of anxiety and fear. I was freed from my childhood demons, the horror of the Vietnam war and the futility of my self-destructive behaviors. I found the solution to all my problems. I now pass this solution on to others, especially those who suffer from alcoholism, drug addiction and compulsive behaviors.

James introduced me to a four-page pamphlet titled *How to Listen to God* and he guided me through the Four Steps as he had taken them in the mid 1930's. These steps removed the blocks which had separated me from the Voice within.

The *How to Listen to God* pamphlet was written in the late 1930's by a Columbus, Ohio Oxford Group member named John Batterson. John attended Group meetings with Dr. Bob Smith, the Akron, Ohio co-founder of the Twelve Step Movement. Even though this guide was used by thousands of people in the 1940's to establish and maintain a two-way communication with God, this important piece of spiritual literature had faded into obscurity in the subsequent decades.

In all of my travels throughout North America studying the great spiritual movements of the Twentieth century, I have only come across one copy of *How to Listen to God*–the one given to me by James Houck. In the past four years, James and I have distributed more than 300,000 copies of this life-changing pamphlet.

What I have experienced during these past four years is nothing short of miraculous. I have watched James Houck "change" more than one hundred thousand lives within the Twelve Step Movement, the Baltimore school system and the Baltimore waterfront.

This is a remarkable story of a man born on a farm in

Walkersville, Maryland on a cold February morning in 1906. As James likes to tell it, "I was born there so I could be close to my mother."

James was raised in this rural community without the benefit of electricity or motorized travel. He spent his formative years "ripping and running" along the East coast. During a meeting in December 1934, the Oxford Group changed his life. For the past sixty-five years, James has been giving away what had been so freely given to him.

My spiritual journey with James began with a telephone call on a Sunday afternoon. I was at home working on a presentation for the Wilson House in East Dorset, Vermont, titled *The Greatest Spiritual Movements of the Twentieth Century.* The seminar was scheduled for the weekend of March 15.

I was sitting at my desk, daydreaming. The weather outside was typical for Tucson, Arizona in midwinter: clear and warm. I was about to set the project aside and take a walk along the ironwood and palo verde lined arroyos down the street when the phone rang. A lady from Western Pennsylvania was on the line. She had news to share.

Her name was Chris. She had just returned home from a Twelve-Step conference in Maryland where she had met a man who claimed to have been sober for more than sixty years. In addition, he told her he had attended Oxford Group meetings with Bill Wilson in the 1930's. His name was James Houck.

I found Chris's comments interesting. Having spent the past four years studying the major spiritual movements of the Twentieth Century, including the Oxford Group and the Twelve Step Movement, I thought I had a good idea who the early members were in each of these organizations. I had conducted extensive research at twenty-two archival collections and had interviewed more than one hundred of the Twelve Step pioneers. Not once had James Houck's name come up.

The thought came to me that James might have gotten a bit senile in his old age. In the past, elderly people had surfaced with all kinds of stories about how they helped start the Twelve Step Movement or assisted with the writing of the "Big Book." Very little, if any, of what they had to say could be verified by the archival records.

I took down James Houck's telephone number and told Chris I would call him. Later that evening, I began to think about James. If he was delusional, it would be best if I stopped him before he had the chance to mislead any more people at these Twelve Step conventions.

The history of the Twelve Step Movement was cloudy enough as it was. Archivists and historians did not need additional unsubstantiated and contradictory information muddying the waters any more than they already were.

That is when I decided to do the Twelve Step community a favor and expose James Houck. I started compiling a list of questions that only someone closely associated with the early days of the Oxford Group and the Twelve Step Movement would be able to answer.

A couple of days later, I called James and introduced myself. He seemed pleasant enough on the phone. He was friendly and appeared to be coherent.

I made an appointment to call him back to pose my

questions. Then, I asked permission to record the conversation. He agreed to my request.

I soon realized that James had an unusual sense of humor. He made the comment that I should call back sooner rather than later. When I asked why, he replied, "Wally, I don't buy green bananas any more."

After completing my list of questions, I called James back on February 27. I made sure he was available for an hour or so. Then I turned the tape recorder on. When James did not have an answer to my first question, I thought, "This is going to be a short interview." I could not have been more mistaken.

Telephone Interview with James Houck

Wally
"This tape is being recorded on Feb 27, 1996. I am talking with James Houck. I hope I pronounced your last name correctly."

James
"That's right. I'm Jim Houck. Hi."

Wally
"Hi. Thanks for taking my call. When we talked last week, you agreed to let me record this conversation for my archives. The tape is running.

"James is 90 years old. He lives in Timonium, Maryland, a suburb of Baltimore. He has a sobriety date in the Oxford Group of December 12, 1934.

"Last week, James told me he probably is the only person

alive today who worked with Bill Wilson in the Oxford Group during the mid 1930's. This is extraordinary news for those of us who are studying this period in history. I am hoping that from this conversation, we will learn more about the spiritual roots of the Twelve Step Movement.

"James, I'd like to start by asking you a few questions about your association with Bill."

James
"Okay. I'm ready."

Wally
"My first question is, 'On what night of the week did you and Bill attend Oxford Group meetings at the Calvary Church in New York City?' "

James
"Wally, I can't answer that. I never attended meetings in New York in the mid 1930's."

Wally
"Then, how did you know Bill Wilson if you didn't go to meetings with him?"

James
"Oh, I did go to meetings with Bill, but in Frederick, Maryland, not New York City."

Wally
"What?"

James
"Bill would come to our meeting in Frederick. He told me

he was staying with a friend who lived in the area. I don't remember the other man's name, but I do remember Bill."

Wally
"Well, I'll be. The other person must have been Fitz Mayo. He had an estate outside of Annapolis. I was there last year. It's a nice place–right on the Chesapeake Bay."

James
"Bill said it was horse property. He spent a lot of time there, especially in the summer."

Wally
"That makes sense. Bill was very poor at the time. I'm sure he would have jumped at the opportunity to spend time at Fitz's estate.

"Well, so much for my prepared questions. I'm going to put this list away and just wing it.

"James, after all these years, how is it that you still remember Bill Wilson?"

James
"Bill was quite a fellow–hard to forget. The first time I met him, I was leading the Saturday night meeting at the Francis Scott Key hotel in Frederick. Bill walked right up to me and said, 'I'm Bill Wilson from New York City. Are you going to have any drunks here tonight?'

"I told him that some of the folks at the meeting may have a drinking problem, but we don't single them out. Bill then said, 'Well, if you have any drunks, send them my way.' That was my introduction to Bill.

"Later, I learned that Bill was obsessed with alcohol. In fact, if you didn't have a drinking problem, he wouldn't even talk to you.

"You see, in the Group we address all aspects of a person's life–everything that keeps an individual separated from God. We don't deal just with alcohol, or drugs, or womanizing, or gambling–we deal with the entire person. It seems to me that Bill never got beyond his alcohol problem."

Wally
"How did you discover the Oxford Group?"

James
"I met the Oxford Group on December 12, 1934 in the very same room at the Frederick, Maryland YMCA where I made a decision for Christ some sixteen years before. In 1918, I attended a church revival there.

"The preacher gave a sermon followed by an altar call. He invited those who were ready to surrender their lives to God to come forward. When nobody took him up on his offer, he asked those who were willing to surrender to raise their hands. I raised my hand thinking nobody would see me, but my high school friends were looking around the room instead of praying. After the service they said, 'We saw you raise your hand. I guess you're going to be a different person now.'

"Well, I didn't feel any different. Even though I had made a decision, I didn't see any reason to change the way I was living. I was surrounded by people who weren't living any differently than I was. I thought it was par for the course.

"Several years later, I joined a church and started teaching

Sunday school. Even then, I saw no relationship between what I talked about on Sunday morning and what I did on Saturday night. All that changed when I met the Oxford Group.

"Louis Wilson (no relation to Bill Wilson) introduced me to the Group. He owned a hosiery mill in Frederick. Louis had already met the Group and he kept inviting me to go to a meeting with him. Finally, one night I accepted his offer.

"This is how it happened. Louis had difficulty seeing at night so he asked me to drive him to a meeting in Baltimore on Friday, December 11. The Washington team was visiting Baltimore and Louis wanted to spend some time with them.

"When one of the Washington team members asked me if I was ready to dedicate my life to God, I told him, 'No thanks.' I was really surprised when he didn't try to pressure me.

"At the Baltimore meeting, Louis invited the Washington team to Frederick the following night. Louis was having labor problems at his mill. He hoped to mend some fences by having the mill laborers and supervisors sit down with several members of the Group.

"Next day, I thought about what had happened in Baltimore. I was impressed by the sheer simplicity of their approach. That evening I did make a decision–a decision that changed my life."

Wally
"How many people were at the meeting?"

James
"About thirty people were there."

Upper Left: The Rising Tide magazine (1937) contained an article on life-changing at the Frederick, Maryland hosiery mill

Upper Right: Carroll Kinsey, who worked at the hosiery mill, attended the Oxford Group meeting with James Houck on Dec. 12, 1934

Lower Right: Carroll Kinsey with Louis Wilson—the man who intro- duced James Houck to the Oxford Group

Lower Left: Hosiery mill employees working the stocking machines

Wally
   "Do you remember any of their names?"

James
   "Oh sure. Many of them became my friends for life."

   "Let's see, from the Washington team there was Skiff Wishard, Cleve Hicks and Randulf Hausland. Randulf was from Norway. He took me through the Steps during the Saturday night meeting. Some of the mill employees were Buzz Rhoderick, Carroll Kinsey and John Wilburn."

Wally
   "How did Randulf take you through the Steps?"

James
   "It was quite straightforward. Randulf and I sat down together. He asked me if he could share something that was troubling him. He said he needed to talk about it in order to get rid of it. I thought this was gutsy for a guy I had never met before. So, I said, 'Okay.'

   "I listened for awhile and then I found myself telling him some of the things in my life I had never shared with anyone. It was different from anything I had ever done before. Here I was telling a total stranger my deepest, darkest secrets. For some reason I felt safe talking to him.

   "After we shared, he asked me if I was ready to surrender these secrets to God. I said, 'yes,' and then we prayed."

Wally
   "Did you get down on your knees, or anything like that?"

James

"No, we just sat there. After we said our prayers, Randulf suggested that I get quiet and listen to God. I was skeptical, to say the least. I didn't believe God could or would talk to me–and I told Randulf so. He suggested I try it anyway.

"Randulf gave me a test I could use to check my thoughts. The test was Honesty, Purity, Unselfishness and Love. According to Randulf, if any of my thoughts passed this test, there was a good chance these thoughts came from God.

"Even though I didn't believe it would work, I gave it a try. I got quiet and listened. The first thought that came to me was to make restitution for something that had happened five years before.

"Wally, I swear there was no way I could have thought of this incident on my own. As far as I was concerned, it was over and done with. I was shocked when the event popped right into my head.

"I realized right then that there was something to this business of listening to God. I told Randulf what I had heard. He suggested that I follow up on the thought, which I did.

"In all, five of us had our lives changed that night. We became the core of the Frederick team.

"At church on Sunday morning, I ran into Brother Geesey. He was a dyed-in-the-wool Christian who led the Tuesday night prayer service. I wanted to tell him about what had happened the night before.

"I told Brother Geesey I had given my life to God the night

before–I was converted. He asked, 'Did a shining light come down from heaven and blind you?' I said, 'No, I didn't see a light.' Shaking his head, he replied, 'I may be wrong, but I don't think you got it.'

"He was trying to tell me the only way to get converted was to experience exactly what he had experienced. He believed you had to see a light. But, I had been changed, no matter what Brother Geesey thought."

Wally
"I am grateful that all of us don't have to see the same light."

James
"Me, too. During the next several weeks I kept listening to God. I made restitution every time it came up in my thoughts. Following the guidance I had received at that Saturday night meeting, I cleared up the trouble I had gotten into five years before when I drove a company car drunk, hit a parked car and left the scene of the accident.

"I spent three nights getting honest with my wife. We were able to put our marriage on a whole new basis–the basis of trusting and relying upon God.

"I made financial restitution for having a jumper on my electric meter. This was a pretty sticky situation because I worked for the local power company at the time.

"Then, I made an amends to a man I had stolen some electrical supplies from some sixteen years before. While I was talking to him, he told me he was having trouble with his marriage. Since I had been honest with him, he decided to go home and get honest with his wife. Later, he told me they were able to work things out.

"In just a couple of weeks, I had seen restitution not only change my life, but the life of another person. This was truly remarkable.

"I always thought restitution was something that you did to clean up your own side of the street. You did it because it made you feel good inside. But, Wally, the important thing–the biggest thing–is what it does for the other person.

"All of us have experienced the power of restitution, but we may not have realized it. At one time or another, we've told someone we were sorry for something we had done. Invariably, the other person will say they had a part in it too.

"What was a vertical barrier between you and the other person has now become a horizontal bridge. A new relationship has been formed between the two of you. Making restitution is an ideal way to convert barriers to bridges. It opens a window into the soul of another person."

Wally
    "What a revelation! I never thought about restitution in terms of changing lives. Did this concept come from Frank Buchman?" (Frank was the founder of the Oxford Group.)

James
    "Yes. Frank incorporated three key elements into the Oxford Group program. They were the Four Standards of Honesty, Purity, Unselfishness and Love; the concept of two-way prayer; and the use of restitution to change lives."

Wally
  "What is two-way prayer?"

James,
  "Bill Wilson, Dr. Bob and the other members of the Oxford Group practiced two-way prayer every day. Bill used it as the basis for the Eleventh Step in the Twelve Step programs." (The Eleventh Step reads: Sought through prayer and meditation to improve our conscious contact with God *as we understood Him*, praying only for knowledge of His will for us and the power to carry that out.)

  "In the Oxford Group, we call it quiet time and guidance. In the Twelve Step program, Bill describes it as prayer and meditation. Basically, it's the same thing.

  "The idea is to set aside time every morning to receive guidance from God. Prayer is talking to God and meditation is listening to God. Most people know how to pray, but very few know how to listen.

  "Just as we pray to God through our minds, God talks to us through our minds. The key to the whole process is to get quiet, write down what you hear and share what you've written with another person.

  "For those who are married, this is usually the husband or wife. For those who aren't, our sharing partner can be a close friend or fellow church member. The important thing is that the person we share with must also be listening to God.

  "I have a pamphlet written by a friend of mine that explains the entire process. I'll send it along to you. It provides step-by-step instructions on two-way prayer. The title of the pamphlet is *How to Listen to God*."

Wally
       "This is definitely something I'd be interested in. When was the pamphlet written?"

James
       "I'm not sure, but it had to have been in the late 1930's. I believe John Batterson gave it to me in 1938."

Wally
       "Who is John Batterson?"

James,
       "He was a minister living in Columbus, Ohio who spent a lot of time with the Akron and Cleveland teams."

Wally
       "Do you think John knew Dr. Bob?"

James,
       "I'm sure he did. He knew all the members in the area.

       "I don't believe I ever met Dr. Bob. In the late 1930's, I spent most of my time with the Washington, D.C. and New York City teams. I didn't make it out to the Midwest until the 1940's. By that time, Dr. Bob had already left the Oxford Group and was involved full time with the Twelve Step Movement."

Wally
       "Did you know any of the other Akron team members?"

James
       "Oh, sure. I knew most of them.

"The Akron group was very active. Some of the key members were Bud Firestone, the son of Harvey Firestone, T. Henry and Clarace Williams, and Henrietta Seiberling.

"In the summer of 1942, Mrs. Henry Ford told Frank he needed to move his team to Mackinac Island. Frank sent in a small group of members who rented the Island House for a dollar a year. At the time, the hotel was unoccupied.

"The facility was in bad shape, so we completely renovated it. We held our first conference there on Labor Day weekend in 1942. We held conferences there from 1942 until the early 1960's."

Wally
"How many of these conferences did you attend?"

James
"I attended all of them."

Wally,
"Who was at the first one?"

James
"I remember that Mrs. Thomas Edison was there, along with the Fords and Jimmy and Ellie Newton. Jimmy was the spark plug for the whole Midwest operation. It was Jimmy and Sam Shoemaker who changed Bud Firestone back in 1931. (Jimmy Newton practiced two-way prayer with such notables as Thomas Edison, Henry Ford, Harvey Firestone and Charles Lindbergh. In 1987, he wrote an autobiography titled *Uncommon Friends*.)
(Sam Shoemaker was the U.S. leader of the Oxford Group in the 1930's. He was the minister of the Calvary Church in New York

City and headed up the team which included Bill Wilson.)

"T. Henry and Clarace Williams and Henrietta Seiberling were there. I did spend a considerable amount of time with them."

Wally
"What can you tell me about Henrietta Seiberling?"

James
"Henrietta was the daughter-in-law of Frank Seiberling. He started the Goodyear and the Seiberling tire companies.

"Henrietta was separated from her husband. She lived, along with her children, in a guest house which was separate from the rest of the Seiberling estate. When she got changed, her guest house became one of the centers for the Akron team."

Wally
"Oh, James, I have so many questions."

James
"I'll answer them as best I can. I try not to talk beyond my own experience. A stream cannot rise higher than its source."

Wally
"James, you are the source of so much information. We must get together again soon. There is so much for me to learn."

James
"It could take years."

Wally
    "I'm ready, if you are."

    "Before we finish this session though, I'd like to know a few more things about the Oxford Group. How well did you know Frank Buchman?"

James
    "I knew Frank fairly well. I wasn't a member of his team, but we did talk many times.

    "Frank's main objective was life-changing. He wasn't concerned so much with saving souls as he was with changing lives. Frank worked within all the churches. He didn't profess any specific beliefs, but rather, he built a program based upon a few universal truths that were an integral part of most religions.

    "He wasn't interested in getting people into a movement. He wanted to get movement into people.

    "What Frank saw then and I still see today, is that most people in the churches never get beyond their own conversion. It is a vital and meaningful part of their religious experience, but, in many instances, their conversion isn't multiplied into the lives of other people. There is no evangelistic outreach.

    "I find the same thing within the Twelve Step Movement. People go to meetings just to stay sober. They never multiply their spiritual experience into the lives of others. This was not the intent of the original Twelve Step program.

    "We need to rekindle that evangelistic spirit of the early days. Buchman's idea was very simple. He said if you want to change the world you have to start with yourself. Everyone wants to see the other fellow change. Every nation wants to see the other nation change. But, every person and every nation is waiting for the other fellow and other nation to begin.

"Buchman always brought the focus back to the individual. He would ask, 'Are you going to let God solve your problems or are you going to try to solve them yourself? What is it going to be–God's will or self will?'

"The way to learn God's will is to take the Steps. Once you've talked to another person and identified the problem, surrendered it to God, made restitution for any damage you've done, and started listening to God for guidance and direction, you are living in the solution. You now have something to pass on to those in need. The process works! It has worked for me and it will work for anyone who is willing to give it a try."

Wally
    "If you're up for it, let's take a couple of minutes to talk about the Oxford Group meetings."

James,
    "Sure, Wally. Let's continue."

"The purpose of the Oxford Group meetings is to establish and maintain a two-way communication with God. Let's start with the concept of God. Sam Shoemaker used to say, 'Turn as much of yourself as you know over to as much of God as you understand.' We have to start our spiritual journey somewhere, so we begin with what we presently believe. Our understanding of God changes as we grow spiritually.

"I know some people would rather use the term, 'higher

power 'than God. The problem with this is a 'higher power' can be just about anything, even a door knob or a lightbulb.

"When we talk about God, we are specifically referring to the God who speaks–the Voice within. This is important, because the Voice within will guide us in our daily affairs if we take the time to listen. I've never had a doorknob or light bulb speak to me. But, God talks to me every day."

Wally
    "Do you think Bill Wilson learned about the Voice within from the Oxford Group?"

James
    "Almost everything in the Twelve Step Movement came from the Oxford Group. The Voice within is a key concept of both programs.

"There are people who don't believe that God can speak. They say something like, 'The voice inside my head isn't God, it's just my conscience.' I tell them, 'Your conscience may be able to show you the difference between right and wrong, but only the Voice of God can show you the difference between two rights.' "

Wally
    "Two rights? What do you mean?"

James
    "At one time or another, we have all stood at a fork in the road. We have a choice to make and both paths appear to be equally right, such as two different job offers or two different places to live. When we listen to God and test our thoughts, we find that God directs us toward the path that is of maximum

benefit to everyone."

Wally
"I see. That's a great example. It gives me a whole new concept of God. If I listen, I will learn God's plan for my life. What an inspirational message."

James
"The overall philosophy of the Oxford Group is to get to the root of the problem which is soul sickness. By judging everything we think, say or do based on the Four Standards, we do a little soul surgery that touches every area of our lives.

"In the Group, we talked very little about alcohol. It was not a big issue even though many members were alcoholics. Rather than talk about drinking, we would talk about how God had changed our lives."

Wally
"In your opinion, who was the most effective speaker in the Oxford Group?"

James
"Sam Shoemaker, of course.

"Sam had an electric personality. He was energetic and full of life. He also had a way of getting right to the heart of the matter.

"Let me tell you a Sam Shoemaker story. After giving a sermon, Sam would stand by the door of the church to get feedback from the congregation. I remember this one Sunday, when Sam had given this particularly powerful message, he asked a little old lady what she thought. She replied politely,

'Oh, Reverend Shoemaker, it was such a lovely sermon. It gave me so much to think about.' Sam replied, 'You're not supposed to think about it, you're supposed to go out and do something about it.' Yes, Sam was very direct and to the point.

Let's say you'd just come back from a house party (an Oxford Group weekend conference). Sam would come up to you and ask, 'What do you see new in your life today that you hadn't seen before?' He would then wait for an answer.

"Since the turn of the century, the Shoemaker family has lived just a few miles from here, at a place called Burnside. Sam moved there in the mid 1950's after his mother passed away.

"I'd gotten to know Sam during his days at the Calvary Church in New York. In the 1930's, he headed up the Oxford Group for the whole country. We remained friends through the years. When he moved to Burnside, we would get together from time to time."

Wally
   "What was Bill Wilson like at the Oxford Group meetings?"

James
   "All Bill ever wanted to talk about was alcohol. He carried this idea with him all the time.

Bill had a falling out with the folks in New York in 1937 when he wanted to hold separate meetings just for people with an alcohol problem. Frank and Sam told him they didn't want to take that approach because the Oxford Group concept was to change the whole person.

That's when Bill left the Oxford Group to work full time

with alcoholics. Keep in mind that not all the alcoholics left with him. Many stayed behind including Rowland Hazard, Victor Kitchen and me.

"However, Bill did take all the principles of the Oxford Group with him. He incorporated these principles into the Twelve Steps. When you read the 'Big Book' you are reading a piece of Oxford Group literature. Just about everything in that book came from the Oxford Group. Bill just dressed it up a bit for the alcoholics."

Wally
"Is there anything else you'd like to say about the meetings?"

James
"Each meeting had a leader with one or more speakers. The leader would open the meeting with a prayer. Then he or she would introduce the speaker or speakers who would talk about how the Oxford Group program had changed their lives. Later on, the leader would conduct a quiet time so everyone in the room could listen to God. Those who had been directed by God to speak would share with the group the guidance they had received. The leader would then close the meeting with The Lord's Prayer.

"After the meeting, people would get together. Some would pair up and go off by themselves so they could talk about those things they didn't feel comfortable sharing with the group. Others would sit around and talk informally about some aspect of life-changing, such as the Four Standards or the Five C's. Are you familiar with the Five C's?"

Wally
"I've heard of them, but I don't think I could recite them off the top of my head."

James,
"They are an integral part of the life-changing process. The Five C's are Confidence, Confession, Conviction, Conversion and Continuance."

Wally,
"How did you learn about the Five C's?"

James,
"During house parties, the Five C's would come up from time to time. People would relate their experiences and then ask those who were new to the program to share how they planned to use the Five C's in their lives.

"The purpose of the Five C's is to multiply your change into the lives of others. It's a simple process.

"There is a pamphlet titled *How Do I Begin?* that explains the whole life-changing process. I'll send you a copy."

Wally
"Thanks, James. I'm looking forward to reading it.

"We've been on the phone for over an hour now. I don't want to wear you out. Maybe we'd better wrap this session up."

James
"You mean we're starting to circle the field."

Wally
    "Yes we are. But, before we close, I would like to know if
you attended the Oxford Group meeting held in Western
Massachusetts during the summer of 1936. According to a
magazine article, there were about ten thousand people there."
(In October 1936, Emily Newell Blair wrote an article for *Good
Housekeeping* titled "The Oxford Group Challenges America.")

James,
    "That house party was an annual event. I started going to
it in 1935. In the winter, we held our meetings at the Red Lion
Inn in Stockbridge Massachusetts. In the summer, we used a
camp just outside of town.

    "In 1936, the total attendance may have been ten thousand,
but they weren't all there at once. The event lasted for seven
days. People would come and go during the week.

    The largest gatherings took place in 1939. I attended all
three of them.

    "The first one was at Madison Square Garden in New York
City. Fourteen thousand people were there. The second one
was at Constitution Hall in Washington, D.C. About five
thousand showed up for that one.

    "The third meeting was at the Hollywood Bowl in Los
Angeles, California. This outdoor theater had thirty thousand
seats and we filled it. Several thousand had to be turned
away."

Wally
    "I read that as many as fifteen thousand people couldn't get
in. That definitely was an overflow crowd."

James

"It was a big night. Movie celebrities were there–flashbulbs were popping everywhere. There were four spotlights at the back of the stage shooting straight up into the sky. They were very powerful–you could see them for miles. The four beams of light represented the Four Standards of Honesty, Purity, Unselfishness and Love.

"It was quite a dramatic sight. Many of the Hollywood movie people helped put that meeting together."

Wally

"I have seen pictures of the event. It's one thing to read about it–it's something else to have actually been there."

James

"Two friends and I drove cross country to be there. It was worth the trip."

Wally

"What was the slogan for that conference? I keep thinking it was something like 'Changing the world, one life at a time.' Does this sound right?"

James

"I don't think that is an Oxford Group slogan. I've never heard the expression used before. It could be a slogan you have developed on your own. Maybe it's guidance from God.

"The slogan for the Hollywood Bowl conference was New Men–New Nations–A New World."

Wally

"Let's make sure I've got it right: New Men–New Nations–

A New World."

James
  "That's it.

  "People constantly talk about changing the world, but they always talk in terms of some distant place. What is our world? It's the people we live with every day. If we can't do something to change those around us, how are we going to change someone thousands of miles away. We have to deal with the basics–we need to change ourselves first. Then we can change our friends and loved ones."

Wally,
  "Before we finish, I'd like for you to touch on the concept of guidance. In the Oxford Group literature, I have read about the importance of a morning meditation. It's also mentioned in the 'Big Book'. But, why do we need to write down what we hear?"

James
  "Writing guidance is the heart of the program. Some people think there is something mystical about writing guidance, but the reason for writing down what we hear is very simple. It's so we won't forget.

  "Buchman used to say, 'The strongest memory is weaker than the palest ink.' It is very important that you write a thought down. It clears your mind for the next thought. Then you aren't hampered by trying to remember the thoughts.

  "At the end of the day, you review what you have written to see if you have followed your guidance. Actually, there is nothing mystical about it at all."

Wally

"James, you have provided me with a considerable amount of new information. In three weeks, I'm conducting a seminar on spirituality at the Wilson House in East Dorset, Vermont. This is where Bill Wilson was born. I would like for you to tell everyone there what you just told me. If I can make the arrangements, would you like to share the podium with me?"

James

"Sure, Wally. I'd love to. Let me know the details and I'll be there. What do you want me to talk about?"

Wally

"I would like you to describe the spiritual roots of the Twelve Step Movement. You know them from first hand experience. In addition, I'd like for you to reminisce about Bill, because the seminar is being held at his birthplace.

"I'll give Bonnie and Ozzie a call to see what they have to say about all this. I think they will jump at the chance to bring someone to the Wilson House who actually attended Oxford group meetings with Bill. (Bonnie and Ozzie Lepper are the proprietors of the Wilson House.)

"This has been a great session. It's hard to believe that we've been on the telephone for an hour and a half. I would certainly like to do this again.

"I truly believe that if the Twelve Step Movement can get back to its spiritual roots, the fellowship will be stronger and more effective in the years ahead. Right now, most members don't have a clue as to where the Twelve Steps came from. At the Wilson House, you are going to change all that, and hopefully change a few lives in the process."

James
"I'd certainly like the opportunity to do that. In the meantime, I'll get these pamphlets in the mail to you."

Wally
"Thank you. I'll be in touch, probably in a day or so about the Wilson House. It will be a small gathering–Bonnie and Ozzie limit the attendance to 100 people. But, they will be coming from all over the country. In addition, the sessions are tape recorded. This way, we'll be able to get your message out to the world. I know something very positive will come of this. It's truly a miracle that you have come into my life at this time."

James
"Thank Chris. She is the one who put us together."

Wally
"I will definitely call her tonight."

James
"Thank you, Wally. I look forward to hearing from you again."

Wally
"Thank you, James. God Bless."

James
"God Bless."

2
The Challenge

Early the next morning, I called the Wilson House to talk to Bonnie and Ozzie Lepper. They are the proprietors of the East Dorset, Vermont country inn where I was to conduct my spiritual workshop on March 15–17. The volunteer who answered the phone turned me over to Bonnie.

Trying to contain my enthusiasm as much as possible, I explained to her I had just talked to a man who attended Oxford Group meetings with Bill Wilson in the 1930's. I had questioned him extensively and believed he was for real. In addition, I thought he could make a valuable contribution to the seminar.

Bonnie said she would discuss this new development with Ozzie and call me back. Within twenty minutes we were on the phone again.

Bonnie opened the conversation with, "Wally, both Ozzie and I are excited about having someone with James' credentials share the podium with you. If he is able to make the trip, we will cover all his expenses. However, we need to know what special arrangements we will have to make to get him here. You said he was 90 years old, didn't you?"

"Yes, that's what he told me. He's 90 years old." I replied.

"Well, that's our concern. Even if his mind is sound, his body may not be. Ozzie thought it would be best to fly him into Albany which is only an hour and a half drive from here. We will meet him at the airport and provide whatever assistance he needs to get him to East Dorset."

Bonnie then provided me with a list of questions to ask James, so the staff and volunteers would know how to take care of him. These questions had to do with his mobility, medical condition and dietary restrictions.

I called James back to let him know Bonnie and Ozzie had agreed to add him to the program. They would cover all costs. James said that was generous of them but it wouldn't be necessary. He would take care of his own expenses.

I felt a bit uneasy, but I knew I had to ask James the questions Bonnie had provided. I told James I did not want to offend him, but because of his age I needed to know a few things about his health so the Wilson House personnel could make the necessary preparations. Jim said, "Fire away."

My first question was, "James, can you walk?"

"Sure, I can walk," he replied. "I can make it at least as far as from my house to the car."

"What do you mean," I asked?

"I'm planning on driving to the Wilson House. I'm going to stop in Stockbridge, Massachusetts to stay at the Red Lion

Inn where we used to hold our Oxford Group meetings in the 1930's."

I quizzed James further. "Are you sure you're up for this? You're ninety years old."

"Oh, sure. I drive all the time. I get around pretty well. I've been blessed with good health."

So much for Bonnie's list of questions. I made sure James did not need any special attention or specific foods during his stay at the Wilson House. He assured me he had no trouble climbing stairs or staying up late. All he asked for was an afternoon nap. I told him we would certainly work around his nap schedule.

Two days later, I received a package in the mail from James. It contained the two pamphlets he described during our telephone conversation. I started with the *How to Listen to God* pamphlet because James told me he wanted to present it at the Wilson House.

I was surprised to find it was four pages long and only took a couple of minutes to read. The content was unprecedented. I immediately realized the significance of this very short dissertation.

Here was the essence of the spiritual ideals I had been studying and writing about for years. The pamphlet contained everything a person needed to know about meditation–the technique of listening to God.

Parts of the pamphlet were familiar–the principles were pure Oxford Group. But, I had never seen anything presented in such an easy-to-understand, concise manner.

The pamphlet opened with a bold statement: listening to God was the most important thing a person could ever learn. This was followed by a challenge to try it. If a person was willing to follow the directions, he or she would establish and maintain a two-way communication with the Voice within–the "God who speaks." It was presented as a guarantee!

The remainder of the pamphlet provided step-by-step instructions on how to listen to God. The author listed eight fundamental points to help present a clear understanding of God. Next, he specified a series of eight steps that, if followed, would put us directly in contact with this Divine Inner Presence. They were: (1) Take Time, (2) Relax, (3) Tune In, (4) Listen, (5) Write, (6) Test, (7) Check and (8) Obey. Next he described what to do if we were blocked off from God or we had mistaken self-thoughts for God thoughts. The pamphlet concluded with the benefits we would receive if we followed this simple formula for two-way prayer.

I said to myself, "This is what I have been searching for all my life. This is the roadmap I have needed to take my spiritual journey to the next level."

I read the pamphlet a second time:

HOW TO LISTEN TO GOD

These are a few simple suggestions for people who are willing to make an experiment. You can discover for yourself the most important and practical thing any human being can ever learn—how to be in touch with God.

All that is needed is the ***willingness to try it honestly***. Every person who has done this consistently and sincerely has found that it really works.

Before you begin, look over these fundamental points. They are true and are based on the experience of thousands of people.

1. God is alive. He always has been and He always will be.

2. God knows everything.

3. God can do anything.

4. God can be everywhere–all at the same time. (These are the important differences between God and us human beings.)

5. God is invisible–we can't see Him or touch Him–but ***God is here.*** He is with you now. He is beside you. He surrounds you. He fills the room or the whole place where you are right now. He is in you now. He is in your heart.

6. God cares very much for ***you***. He is interested in you. He has a plan for your life. He has an answer for every need and problem you face.

7. God will tell you all that you ***need*** to know. He will not always tell you all that you ***want*** to know.

8. God will help you do anything that He asks you to do.

9. Anyone can be in touch with God, anywhere and at any time, ***if the conditions are obeyed.***

    These are the conditions:

    - To be quiet and still
    - To listen
    - To be honest about every thought that comes
    - To test the thoughts to be sure that they come from God
    - To obey

So, with these basic elements as a background, here are specific suggestions on how to listen to God:

1. *Take Time*
Find some place and time where you can be alone, quiet and undisturbed. Most people have found that the early morning is the best time. Have with you some paper and pen or pencil.

2. *Relax*
Sit in a comfortable position. Consciously relax all your muscles. Be loose. There is no hurry. There needs to be no strain during these minutes. God cannot get through to us if we are tense and anxious about later responsibilities.

3. *Tune In*
Open your heart to God. Either silently or aloud, just say to God in a natural way that you would like to find His plan for your life—you want His answer to the problem or situation that you are facing just now. Be definite and specific in your request.

4. *Listen*
Just be still, quiet, relaxed and open. Let your mind go "loose." Let God do the talking. Thoughts, ideas, and impressions will begin to come into your mind and heart. Be alert and aware and open to every one.

5. *Write!*
Here is the important key to the whole process. Write down everything that comes into your mind. *Everything*. Writing is simply a means of recording so that you can remember later. *Don't* sort out or edit your thoughts at this point.

Don't say to yourself:
This thought isn't important;
This is just an ordinary thought;
This can't be guidance;
This isn't nice;
This can't be from God;
This is just me thinking, etc.

Write down everything that passes through your mind:
Names of people;
Things to do;
Things to say;
Things that are wrong and need to be made right.

Write down everything:
   Good thoughts–bad thoughts;
   Comfortable thoughts–uncomfortable thoughts;
   "Holy" thoughts–"unholy" thoughts;
   Sensible thoughts–"crazy" thoughts.

Be Honest! Write down ***everything***. A thought comes quickly, and it escapes even more quickly unless it is captured and put down.

6.   ***Test***
When the flow of thoughts slows down, stop. Take a good look at what you have written. ***Not every thought we have comes from God.*** So we need to test our thoughts. Here is where the written record helps us to be able to look at them.

a)   Are these thoughts completely ***honest, pure, unselfish and loving?***
b)   Are these thoughts in line with our duties to our family, to our country?
c)   Are these thoughts in line with our understanding of the teachings found in our spiritual literature?

7.   ***Check***
When in doubt and when it is important, what does another person who is living two-way prayer think about this thought or action? More light comes in through two windows than one. Someone else who also wants God's plan for our lives may help us to see more clearly.

Talk over together what you have written. Many people do this. They tell each other what guidance has come. This is the secret of unity. There are always three sides to every question–your side, my side, and the right side. Guidance shows us which is the right side–not who is right, but what is right.

8.   ***Obey***
Carry out the thoughts that have come. You will only be sure of guidance as you go through with it. A rudder will not guide a boat until the boat is moving. As you obey, very often the results will convince you that you are on the right track.

9.   ***Blocks?***
What if I don't seem to get any definite thoughts? God's guidance is as freely available as the air we breathe. If I am not receiving thoughts when I listen the fault is not Gods.

Usually it is because there is something ***I will not do:***
   something wrong in my life that I will not face and make right;

a habit or indulgence I will not give up;
a person I will not forgive;
a wrong relationship in my life I will not give up;
a restitution I will not make;
something God has already told me to do that I will not obey.

Check these points and be honest. Then try listening again.

10. *Mistakes*

Suppose I make a mistake and do something in the name of God that isn't right? Of course we make mistakes. We are humans with many faults. However, ***God will always honor our sincerity.***

He will work around and through every honest mistake we make. He will help us make it right. ***But remember this!*** Sometimes when we do obey God, someone else may not like it or agree with it. So when there is opposition, it doesn't always mean you have made a mistake. It can mean that the other person doesn't want to know or to do what is right.

Suppose I fail to do something that I have been told and the opportunity to do it passes? There is only one thing to do. Put it right with God. Tell Him you're sorry. Ask Him to forgive you, then accept His forgiveness and begin again. God is our Father—He is not an impersonal calculator. He understands us far better than we do.

11. *Results*

We never know what swimming is like until we get down into the water and try. We will never know what this is like until we sincerely try it.

Every person who has tried this honestly finds that a wisdom, not their own, comes into their minds and that Power greater than human power begins to operate in their lives. It is an endless adventure.

There is a way of life, for everyone, everywhere. Anyone can be in touch with the living God, anywhere, anytime, ***if we fulfill His conditions:***

> ***When man listens, God Speaks.***
> ***When man obeys, God Acts.***

This is the law of prayer.

God's plan for this world goes forward through the lives of ordinary people who are willing to be governed by Him.

John E. Batterson

The next morning, I started practicing the principles found in the pamphlet. I used a white, college-ruled notepad to record my thoughts and a white, three-ring binder to store them.

I immediately realized this was a spiritual technique I had not tried before. For years, I had attempted to empty my mind of thoughts. The idea of letting the thoughts flow, writing them down and then testing them to separate the God thoughts from the self-thoughts was revolutionary. Writing and following guidance became part of my daily routine.

On the evening of March 14, I caught the "red-eye" out of Phoenix to New York City. I arrived at the JFK airport right in the middle of the morning commute. I rented a car and headed north. I was grateful that, for the most part, I was traveling against the flow of traffic. Not being a fan of bumper-to-bumper gridlock, I got out of the city as quickly as I could.

I was in great spirits, having completed my preparations for the Wilson House seminar a couple of hours before leaving for the airport. My outlines were complete and I had shot about three hundred slides for the seminar.

I had been conducting historical and spiritual presentations for several years now. During this time, I had developed a technique for making each seminar new and different. I would choose various slides from each topic to be discussed, load them into carousels and then record the slide sequence. As soon as a slide was shown, I would talk about its historical or spiritual significance. This way, I did not need a prepared text for the seminar, only a list of the slides.

After a six-hour drive through Connecticut, Massachusetts

Upper: The Wilson House in East Dorset, VT where the author met James Houck on March 15, 1996.

Lower: Left to right--Wally Paton, Bonnie Lepper, Ozzie Lepper, James Houck (Bonnie and Ozzie are the proprietors for the Wilson House.)

and southern Vermont, I arrived at the Wilson House. I had driven through snow flurries in the Berkshires and Green Mountains–typical March weather for New England.

When I pulled up in front of the Wilson House, about thirty of the one hundred attendees were already there. They all wanted to know, "Who is this James Houck?" I described what little I knew about him.

Just being at the Wilson House was a spiritual experience. It was my third trip to this very special country inn located at the base of Mount Aeolus in the Green Mountain National Forest.

East Dorset is a step back in time. With a population of about 300, this idyllic New England community consists of two streets and fifty homes. The only businesses are a small country store on Highway 7 which bypasses the town and the Wilson House located at the intersection of the two streets.

When Bonnie and Ozzie Lepper purchased the Wilson House in October 1986, the twenty-eight room structure was in total disrepair: it was vacant and uninhabitable. They were on a pilgrimage to East Dorset to visit Bill Wilson's grave site. They saw the condition of the building and realized it would be a tragedy to let this historically significant landmark disappear. Two days later they bought it.

The Leppers returned to Westport, Connecticut and sold everything they owned. Next, they formed a nonprofit foundation to renovate the building. With the help of volunteers, they spent the next several years rebuilding and restoring. In 1990, they opened the Wilson House as a country inn. Visitors from all over the world have made the journey to East Dorset to spend time in the house where Bill Wilson was born and raised.

Bonnie and Ozzie have dedicated their lives to the Wilson House. When they are not preparing meals, cleaning rooms, cultivating the garden or taking care of the farm animals, they entertain their guests with guided tours and fascinating stories about the Wilson family. To help cover renovation expenses, they host spiritual workshops and seminars. My presentation was one of these special events.

I unloaded the rental car and settled into my guest room upstairs. I engaged myself in some minor busywork while I awaited James' arrival. As the time approached, I became more and more anxious to meet this man who had first-hand knowledge about several lost pieces of spiritual history. I was not alone. Everyone in the house was waiting and wondering in anxious anticipation.

James said he would arrive at three o'clock. Sure enough, at three, James pulled up in a late model Chrysler, a big, comfortable boat of a car. He jumped out, bounded up the steps, introduced himself and proceeded to change the lives of everyone in the house.

Even though he did not say or do anything out of the ordinary, the results were electrifying. Here was a life-changer who had been honing his skills since 1934. It was evident to all that James was a very special man who had a tremendous love of life which radiated to everyone around him. Just being in his presence changed some of us. For others it was a gentle touch, a warm smile, or maybe a conversation or two that brought about the conversion. Before the weekend was over, everyone had been transformed.

James was a devout listener, with an uncanny ability to hear what had not been said. He was adept at answering the silent questions and the unexpressed pleas for help.

After a light meal, James took a nap. He needed to rest before the Friday night session.

That evening, I had James speak first because I still was unsure of his capabilities. I figured if he was unprepared or unable to speak coherently in public, I would be able to regroup and conduct the rest of the seminar on my own.

It did not take me long to realize that James knew what he was talking about. He was so much at peace with the world that you could see the pure light of God shining through him.

He described in great detail how he had lived his life since Dec. 12, 1934 based on two-way prayer and the Four Standards of Honesty, Purity, Unselfishness and Love. He used these standards to test the guidance he received during his "quiet time" and to separate God directed versus self-directed thoughts and actions.

He closed his part of the Friday night session by explaining the *How to Listen to God* pamphlet. Since I was already practicing two-way prayer and believed in the value of the pamphlet, I had made copies beforehand. As I passed them out, James asked everyone to follow the pamphlet's directions on Saturday morning and let him know what happened.

James joined the Saturday sessions at about ten o'clock. He came right up to the podium and requested a couple minutes of time. He asked those who had practiced two-way prayer this morning to raise their hands. Four or five hands went up.

James said he would like to meet with each of them during the day to share guidance and discuss God's plan for their lives.

I had never seen anything like this. James was directly following up on the challenge he issued on Friday night. He encouraged those who had not practiced two-way prayer to give it a try, and he offered to be a sharing partner for those who had. It was a call to action. I knew we were all going to learn something from his attempt to motivate the attendees to do something they had not tried before.

James then sat in the back of the room away from the area where the sessions were held. Throughout the day, people would sit down with him to talk, share or ask questions.

Many of the attendees had come to hear lectures rather than practice spiritual exercises. When James asked them to get involved, they were skeptical, but as the day wore on, they began to feel enthusiastic about sharing guidance with James. I realized that James was changing the mood of the seminar, one life at a time.

During the course of the day, I presented material on the historical and philosophical aspects of various spiritual moments of the twentieth century. During my presentation on the Oxford Group I turned the floor over to James. He described the *How to Listen to God* pamphlet again. This time he described how the Oxford Group and the Twelve Step Movement used this technique during the 1930's and 1940's.

That evening I talked about my personal spiritual journey. At 9:30 p.m., I was just about to bring the session to a close when James came forward and asked to speak. I handed the microphone to him, again not knowing what was going to happen.

James issued a second challenge. He asked everyone to use the *How to Listen to God* pamphlet to practice "quiet time and guidance" on Sunday morning. Taking the challenge to the next level, he told everyone to write down their guidance and bring it to the Sunday morning meeting.

I was caught completely off guard. No one had ever done anything like this at a spiritual retreat before, at least, not at any retreat I was familiar with. It was obvious that James was quite serious about everyone practicing two-way prayer. But, we had not discussed this beforehand and I had three hours of material already planned for the Sunday session.

After closing the meeting, I got together with James. I told him there was very little time available on Sunday and asked him how much he needed. He answered, "I'll leave this up to you. God has all the time in the world for us. What it comes down to is how much time do we have for God?"

He went on to explain that listening to God can be difficult for some and outright frightening for others. We needed to provide everyone the opportunity to experience two-way prayer. It would be a tragedy to give the attendees the directions and then let them try to figure them out on their own. Besides, it would be a way to show the cynics that the process really worked.

On Sunday morning I prayed for guidance and wrote down what I heard. The Voice within directed me to take one hour of material out of my Sunday morning presentation.

I adjusted my schedule and finished my remarks at eleven

Upper Left: Red Lion Inn, Stockbridge, MA (James attended Oxford Group meetings at this location in the 1930's)

Upper Right: James and Wally at the Wilson House, East Dorset, VT for a "Converting Barriers to Bridges" seminar (April 1999)

Bottom: James at an informal social gathering "holding court" with some of those interested in learning more about two-way prayer (April 1999)

o'clock. At that time, I turned the microphone over to James.

James once again asked how many had practiced "quiet time and guidance" that morning. This time about a dozen hands went up. I could see that many in the room started to feel uneasy about being put on the spot about two-way prayer. James put them at ease when he suggested a "quiet time" right there in the meeting room. He asked for five minutes of silence so everyone could listen to God and write down what they heard.

James opened the guidance session with a joke:

"A man was walking down the street in New York City with a violin under his arm. He approached a person passing by to ask directions.

"Excuse me, he said. Can you tell me how to get to Carnegie Hall?

"The passerby replied, Practice, man, practice."

James then explained the importance of practicing two-way prayer on a daily basis. He said guidance would take each of us to a new level of spiritual awareness and free us from our problems. Emphasizing that all problems arise from self, he stressed that all solutions come from God.

James told us how guidance had not only changed his own life, but the lives of people around him. He related a story about how he had saved a man's marriage just by following guidance and making restitution to him.

Next James set the stage by thanking those who had

already shared guidance with him during the course of the weekend. As he had explained to his sharing partners, guidance is normally shared with one other person, a person who is also practicing two-way prayer. Nothing confidential or too personal was to be shared with the Group.

To break the ice, James read his guidance. He pulled a small, spiral-wound notebook from an inside pocket of his suit coat. He flipped to the last page of handwritten notes and shared what he had written.

Next, he turned the microphone over to me. I read to the group what I had written about giving James the opportunity to conduct a guidance session. I also read something one of the Benedictine monks, Brother Robert had quoted during a prayer service at the Weston Priory Monastery at five o'clock that morning. The passage was from the book *Addiction and Grace*:

> "God creates us out of love, and this love draws us toward God by means of our deepest desires. Yet we are created with free will, and this freedom allows us to choose to be for or against God, life and love.

> "Grace is our only hope for dealing with addiction, the only power that can truly vanquish its destructiveness. Grace is the absolute expression of perfect love. It is a gift that we are free to accept, reject or ignore.

> "We will never turn to God as long as we are handling things well enough by ourselves. However, our most powerful addictions will cause us to defeat ourselves, bringing us to the rock bottom realization that we cannot master everything. It is addiction that brings us to our knees and ultimately to God."

(Brother Robert, 5:00 a.m. vigil 3/17/96 paraphrased)

I thought it was more than coincidence that Brother Robert had chosen this day to read a passage about how addiction separates us from God. Here we were several hours later trying to move beyond our addictions, afflictions and compulsive behaviors in order to get reconnected.

James then asked those that felt comfortable to come forward and share what they had written during their "quiet time." He was specifically interested in what God had to say about carrying the message of two-way prayer to others.

The first person to the podium was a young man who shared that by listening to God he had witnessed a new way of living. He had written, "Let My light come shining through."

A woman from Canada knew she had been directed to this seminar to enhance the effectiveness of her service work. She received guidance to start a meeting in her home based on the pamphlet.

Several others shared how burdens had been lifted and fears overcome as the result of listening to God. They felt relief and release by writing down what they heard in their moments of silent contemplation.

Then a man stood up and cried for several minutes. After gathering his composure, he told his story:

> "I live about an hour from here. I have been in recovery for more than ten years, but I found myself getting more and more depressed. I was seriously considering suicide. Then on Friday I heard a Voice

that told me to come to the Wilson House. It said I would find what was missing from my life here. I didn't even know there was a seminar going on.

"Even though I didn't get here until Saturday afternoon, my life will never be the same. Yes, listening to God is the answer I have been looking for all these years. Thank you James for saving my life."

It was obvious that God had brought this man to us. Listening to the Voice within had changed his life. Telling his story changed ours.

James closed the session with a plea to continue listening to and following guidance. He asked us to pass along what we had learned to our friends and loved ones. He closed with a prayer of thanks that God had been revealed through us and then sent us on our way to transform the world.

After the close of the seminar, many of the participants came forward to tell me that James Houck and the *How to Listen to God* pamphlet had truly made a difference. Bonnie and Ozzie immediately booked James and me for a return engagement the following year.

I had seen a life-changer at work. I needed to learn everything I possibly could from this quiet, unassuming spiritual giant. I decided to become a student of the Oxford Group program and do everything I could to bring this forgotten piece of spiritual history back into the hearts and lives of everyone I met.

As soon as I returned to Tucson, I started searching the

spiritual and religious literature for evidence of two-way prayer. I was amazed how much there was, now that my eyes had been opened.

During the next several months I was on the telephone with James about once a week. He challenged me to find a local sharing partner to share guidance with on a daily basis. I thought this would be easy enough to do, but this did not turn out to be the case.

I was amazed to find that not one of my Tucson friends was practicing two-way prayer. Even after I explained the pamphlet to them, they were not interested in becoming a sharing partner.

I expressed my disappointment to James. He encouraged me to continue my search because he had received guidance there was something for me to learn from all this.

I then started talking about two-way prayer with just about everyone I came in contact with, both in person and over the phone. After searching for a sharing partner for more than three months, I finally found someone who understood what I was talking about.

His name was Derek and he lived in Northern California. After listening to an audio tape of one of my archival presentations, he called to ask me to clarify some of the statements I had made.

After discussing history for a while I asked Derek if he practiced two-way prayer. He said he had been listening to the Inner Voice and writing guidance for several years. The technique had been presented to him during a spiritual workshop on mysticism. I asked him if I could share my guidance with him from time to time. He agreed. I now had my first sharing partner besides James Houck.

I continued to search for others with whom to share guidance, at first to no avail. Derek and I continued to share guidance for the remainder of 1996 and into 1997, without ever meeting face to face.

We finally met at a Twelve-Step conference held in Phoenix in February 1997. James Houck was one of the speakers at this event.

During the conference, James, Derek and I discussed the difficulty of getting people to listen to God. We concurred that once they started listening, most of them quickly saw the benefit of this spiritual exercise and would continue to do it. The problem seemed to be convincing people to try it in the first place.

During a sharing session several months after this conference, I reported to James that I thought we had made a breakthrough. I was to speak at a major spiritual event in the Midwest in August. I had received permission to make a presentation based on the *How to Listen to God* pamphlet. Since several thousand would to be in attendance, I believed it would be an ideal time to carry the message of two-way prayer.

James asked me to issue a challenge. He thought it would be beneficial to know how many people actually practiced "quiet time and guidance."

I was fascinated by James' curiosity and I agreed to try it. I realize now, James wanted me to see for myself just how many people were listening to God.

I put my presentation onto slides so everyone could follow along and made 500 copies of the *How to Listen to God* pamphlet. The convention committee provided me with an airline ticket that put me in Omaha Nebraska on Friday afternoon.

I was to speak at the Saturday morning meeting. I arrived early to make sure the equipment was operating properly.

At ten thirty, the crowd was settling in–twelve hundred or so. They had been milling about, exchanging pleasantries, sharing stories and enjoying the energy of the convention atmosphere. Now, they were finding seats and quieting down–waiting for the presentation to begin.

I started reading from a meditation book to take my mind off the anxiety that was starting to build. Until a few years ago, I was absolutely terrified of people and could not speak in public. Even though God had miraculously removed that fear, I still felt a bit uneasy when I looked at the size of the crowd.

This was a typical convention–a celebration of life, expressed through food, fun and fellowship, plus a series of speaker meetings. Most of the speakers were "professionals" who traveled from convention to convention telling their stories. It was unusual to have a historical presentation at one of these conventions, but here I was, getting ready to talk about the evolution of two-way prayer.

My anxiety continued to build. I then realized I had forgotten to pray. I walked to the back of the stage and stepped behind the curtain.

I repeated the prayer I had been saying for years, ever since I was asked to speak in Cleveland, Ohio in 1989. I dropped to my knees and said:

> "God, I can't do this by myself. I need your help. Please speak through me. Let my words be your words. Amen."

I began to have second thoughts about challenging the crowd. After all, they had come to sit, listen and be entertained. Maybe asking 1,800 people to take action was too much. But, I had told James that I would ask the questions. Now it was time for me to walk through the fear and follow up on my commitment to James.

The meeting started. After an opening prayer, the chairperson introduced me.

I spent the first couple minutes thanking the committee for the invitation. Next, I provided an overview of my presentation. Then I moved to the questions.

> "Before I begin, I need to get a better understanding of where this group is in terms of two-way prayer. Please help me out, if you will.

> "My first question is, How many of you practiced prayer and meditation this morning"?

More than 1,000 hands went up. I was impressed.

> "Thank you. Now, how many of you wrote down what God had to say"?

Not a single hand remained raised. This was a revelation.

Here were more than one thousand people who said they practiced prayer and meditation, but not one of them wrote down what they heard. Now I knew why it had taken so long to find a sharing partner.

Written guidance was an integral part of the original Oxford Group and Twelve Step program. I now realized what James was trying to do. He knew the practice of listening to God had become a lost spiritual practice. Entire generations of Americans had become disconnected.

I spent the next hour trying to get the audience reconnected to God by taking them through the *How to Listen to God* pamphlet. I explained where the pamphlet came from and why it was such an integral part of the initial success of the Oxford Group and the Twelve Step Movement. I read my guidance to them so they could see what I was talking about. I then told several stories about how two-way prayer had changed my life and the lives of several people around me.

I closed my presentation by issuing the challenge James Houck had issued to me at the Wilson House: become a sharing partner and practice two-way prayer. It will change your life.

The audience response was mixed. Some of the attendees moved onto the next session or back to their conversations in the hall. Others responded to my call to action and came forward to receive a copy of the *How to Listen to God* pamphlet. In the next half hour I handed out all 500 copies.

James was right. There was a great need for an answer to the problem of "soul sickness." Getting the pamphlet into the hands of those who wanted to practice two-way prayer was a beginning:

> "At the start, this was all we needed to commence spiritual growth, to effect our first conscious relationship with God."

3

More is Revealed

In the fall of 1996, I contacted Ohio Wesleyan University which is located just north of Columbus, Ohio. In 1972, Benjamin Forbes donated seventeen boxes of the rarest of Oxford Group archival materials to the university. Since then, the boxes had been in storage at the main library.

Benjamin Forbes owned the Forbes Chocolate Company in Cleveland, Ohio. He was an Oxford Group member who, throughout the 1930's, attended meetings and house parties with Dr. Bob Smith, the Akron, Ohio co-founder of the Twelve Step Movement and John Batterson, the author of the *How to Listen to God* pamphlet.

I wanted to find out if there were any items in the Benjamin Forbes collection that could shed light on the spiritual linkage between the Oxford Group and the Twelve Step Movement. The seventeen boxes had not been opened since they were donated because the money to catalog and preserve the collection was not available. I was the first person to open the boxes and copy the contents. The archives contained Oxford Group books, pamphlets, newsletters, photographs, personal letters and notes.

The personnel at the Ohio Wesleyan library were gracious hosts. They provided table space, copy machines, a light table and after hours access. I spent five days duplicating as much of the collection as possible.

In one of the boxes, I found numerous pocket sized notepads which contained Benjamin's guidance for almost twenty years. They were identical to the notepads still used by James Houck today.

It is one thing to read the Oxford Group literature pertaining to "quiet time and guidance," it is something else to find written evidence that someone actually conducted his business and personal life based on the guidance he received from God. Before me were the intimate details of a man who practiced two-way prayer on a daily basis.

In another box, I found fifty pages of Benjamin's hand written notes from various Oxford Group house parties. Much of the material dealt with the Oxford Group Four Steps and life-changing. Anne Smith, the wife of Dr. Bob Smith, led one of the meetings on two-way prayer. John Batterson was involved in many of these spiritual events.

On Friday, I left Ohio Wesleyan with more than 9,000 copies and several hundred photographs. I drove straight to the Cleveland airport to pick up James Houck who had flown in from Baltimore to meet Sue Smith Windows, Dr. Bob and Anne Smith's daughter. Even though I had been in weekly telephone contact with James during the past eight months, this was the first time we had been together since the Wilson House in East Dorset, Vermont.

James had known many of the members of the Akron team,

but he had never met either Dr. Bob or Anne Smith. He wanted to meet Dr. Bob's daughter, so I arranged for them to get together on the weekend following my trip to Ohio Wesleyan. "Gratitude Sunday," a memorial service for Dr. Bob was also scheduled for this weekend.

James and Sue had dinner together on both Friday and Saturday nights. On Saturday afternoon, I gave James a tour of the important Oxford Group sights: the Mayflower Hotel where some of the Oxford Group house parties were held; the Episcopal Church where Rev. Tunks, an Oxford Group supporter, preached; the Akron City and St Thomas Hospitals where Dr. Bob practiced; the gatehouse where Henrietta Seiberling lived; and the home of T. Henry and Clarace Williams where Group meetings were hosted. In addition, we took a tour of Dr. Bob and Anne Smith's home on 855 Ardmore Avenue. The property had been purchased and renovated by a foundation as a tribute to the co-founder of the Twelve Step Movement.

On Saturday morning, James and I sat down for breakfast at the restaurant next to the motel. After ordering our meals, James asked me to share guidance with him. Because I had overslept, I did not have the time to conduct a "quiet time."

In the eight months since I first met James, I had been practicing two-way prayer on a regular basis. An early morning "quiet time" had become part of my daily routine. But, during this road trip, I had been somewhat negligent about checking in with God before starting each day. Schedules and appointments were set and, for the most part, I just went through each day as it had been planned ahead of time.

I brought some of the material from the Benjamin Forbes

collection with me to breakfast. I was looking forward to getting James' input as to the historical significance of some of the items I had found. I even had several letters written by James to Benjamin Forbes and to the Ohio Wesleyan University pertaining to the donated material.

But, all this would have to wait. First, James wanted to know what God's plan was for me this day. And to think, I had not even taken the time to find out.

I felt embarrassed as I tried to explain why I had not found time for God this morning. I reverted back to an old behavior of making excuses. I said, "James, I was about to get quiet when I realized how late it was. Besides my guidance book was in the car and I didn't have time to get it." The excuses sounded pretty thin, even as I was making them.

James just smiled and said, "It's okay, Wally. We can take time now to get quiet and listen. But before we do, I want to share my guidance with you. I didn't have my guidance book with me, either." Then, James pulled an envelope out of his suit coat inner pocket. He had written his guidance on the back of a piece of hotel stationary.

I immediately realized that James was a very prudent and merciful teacher. He had shown me, with a simple yet effective example, just how important daily guidance was to him. First, he had found the time for God, even with our hectic schedules, and second, he had used whatever was available to put his guidance on paper.

I reached for a paper napkin to write on. James said a prayer asking God to reveal Himself. I started listening and wrote down what I heard. It was difficult to remain focused because of all the noise. We remained quiet until our meals arrived. James blessed the food, and we shared our guidance over oatmeal and scrambled eggs.

That experience was another turning point. Now every time I get rushed in the morning, I find the Inner Voice saying, "What, no time for God?" That is when I stop whatever I am doing, say a prayer of thanks and ask God to direct my thinking. It is amazing how God is always there anytime I reach out and invite the Holy Spirit into my thoughts.

James and Sue Windows were inseparable that weekend. They spent much of their time talking about the Oxford Group program as they saw it being practiced in the mid 1930's. Sue confirmed that "quiet time and guidance" was a daily routine in the Smith household. Anne faithfully wrote her guidance and shared it every morning. Dr. Bob also was a solid believer in guidance, though not as faithful as Anne about writing it down.

James spoke at the memorial service at Dr. Bob's House on Sunday afternoon. Sue was at his side the entire time. After the service, James and Sue were getting ready to say goodbye when I noticed Sue was crying. I went up to her and asked if anything was wrong. She looked up at me and said, "Wally, everything is fine. These are tears of joy. I can't remember when I've been happier. You see, James talks just like my Dad. I haven't heard anyone talk like this in almost fifty years."

I cannot think of any greater testimonial to the authenticity of the James Houck message than to have Dr. Bob's daughter say that he and Dr. Bob spoke the same language and practiced the same program. I told Sue that I would bring James back with me the following year so they could visit again.

As fate would have it, I was able to make good on my

Upper: James Houck with Sue Smith Windows, daughter of Dr. Bob Smith, the Akron, Ohio co-founder of the Twelve Step Movement

Lower: James Houck speaking at Gratitude Sunday, a memorial service for Dr. Bob on Nov. 17, 1996. Seated to the right of James is Sue Smith Windows.

promise to Sue. In November 1997, James and I returned to Akron to spend a day with Sue. This time James and I were on our way from a *Back to Basics* seminar in Dayton, Ohio. We were flying out of Cleveland on Monday morning.

The response to our spiritual message in Dayton had been overwhelmingly positive. Looking back upon the events of that weekend, I now realize the Dayton, Ohio sessions were a major turning point in my spiritual journey. Six hundred people had turned out on Friday night to listen to James speak about the spiritual roots of the Twelve Step Movement and two hundred returned the following day to learn how to listen to God.

The first session on Saturday started at nine o'clock in the morning. By four o'clock in the afternoon everyone had taken the Steps: Surrender, Sharing, Restitution and Guidance.

We began by assigning everyone a sharing partner, a person with whom to discuss an assets and liabilities checklist as part of the Sharing Step and to share what they had heard during a "quiet time" as part of the Guidance Step. During the final session, the participants had the opportunity to share with the Group how two-way prayer had changed their lives.

Sharing with the group was optional. We introduced this part of the program in the following manner:

> "Last session, we asked you to meditate during the break and write down the guidance you received. We realize this is a very personal matter and that your guidance is normally shared with only one other individual who is in two-way communication with God. But, if your guidance is not too intimate or confidential, we ask that you consider sharing what you have written with the

Group. We invite you to demonstrate, to those who
may still be skeptical, that God really does 'disclose
Himself to us.' "

By the fall of 1997, we had been conducting these sessions
for over a year. During this time, we had witnesses thousands
of miracles–lives that had been changed as the direct result of
learning how to listen to God. The results in Dayton were just
as remarkable as previous workshops, only more so. This was
the largest group we had ever taken through the Steps. It
demonstrated that we could successfully take large numbers of
people through the process in one day.

Until Dayton, we were not sure if this program, which was
originally intended for the living room or kitchen table, would
work on a mass scale. But it did work. Participants crowded
the floor microphone to share with everyone in the audience
and with those who would be listening to the audio tapes for
years to come, how the Steps and two-way prayer had given
them a new way of living. Addictions were removed, burdens
lifted, shame and guilt erased. These difficulties were replaced
with faith, knowledge of God's will and hope for the future.

The mood of the room followed the same pattern we had
seen previously with the smaller groups. During the Surrender
Step, the predominant mood was skepticism. This changed to
fear as we prepared the attendees to discuss their character
liabilities as part of the Sharing Step. After the one-on-one
sharing sessions during the two-hour lunch break, fear was
replaced with a sense of relief and well-being. Then, during the
Guidance Step, the overall feeling was pure ecstacy. I could
definitely feel the presence of God in the room, especially as
people came forward to share their guidance.

James and I left the workshop with a renewed faith that we

were doing God's will and that these seminars were making a real difference in the world. Lives had been changed, and these people were now in a position to change others.

We had a quiet dinner with the Dayton, Ohio team leaders followed by a short guidance session. Each of us shared what we planned to do to strengthen and solidify the conversion experiences we had witnessed during the workshop. We also discussed how best to carry the message of two-way prayer to those still in need.

Our hosts then drove us back to the hotel. Since, we had to be in Akron early the next day, we thought it was best to say our good-byes and put James to bed.

Besides, we were exhausted. We needed to get recharged for the next day's activities. James, at 91 years of age, certainly needed his sleep. So did the rest of us.

As we turned in, it began to snow. Soon everything was white.

After "quiet time and guidance" over breakfast, we were on our way. I sat in the passenger's seat, with James in the back. Part of my guidance that morning had been to gather some biographical information on James. I had my tape recorder with me. I handed James the microphone and from the front seat I conducted the following interview:

Wally
"This tape is being recorded on November 16, 1997. I am with James Houck. We are being driven from Dayton to Akron, Ohio on Sunday Morning. James, we have a couple of hours before we get to Dr. Bob's House for the 'Gratitude Sunday' service. I'd like to take some time to get some biographical

information on you for the *How to Listen to God* book I'm writing. What do you say, are you up for it?"

James
   "Sure, Wally. What would you like to know?"

Wally
   "Let's start with your family and childhood experiences."

James
   "I was born on a cold wintery night in Walkersville, Maryland on February 21, 1906. I was born there so I could be close to my mother."

Wally
   "Now that's humorous. You do have a special gift."

James
   "What do you mean, Wally? I'm just telling you how it was."

Wally
   "Sure, James. Let's keep going."

James
   "My mother's name was Virginia; my father's name was Charles. I was the youngest of six children, three brothers and two sisters.

   "The first born was my brother Charles, Jr. The next oldest was my sister Isabelle, followed by Elizabeth who died of diphtheria in childhood. The twins James and William were next, but they also died of diphtheria when they were about two or three years old. I was the last, named after the twins, James William.

"My father was a farmer, and my grandfather was the president of a bank. My grandfather financed farms and owned several of them himself. He gave one of the farms to my father. It was located about three miles from Walkersville, in a town called Ceresville, which was four miles from a town called Frederick. I lived there until I was twelve years old. Our family grew corn and wheat on the farm."

Dandelion Wine

"My mother used to drink dandelion wine. One day I got into her wine and began to drink it. I liked it so much I began to drink her wine on a regular basis, then fill the bottles up with water so she wouldn't know any wine was missing.

"On the first day of school, I put a pint of dandelion wine in my lunch pail. Since I was drinking it like it was Coca-Cola, I thought it would be okay to take it to class. I was very disappointed when they took it away from me. But I continued to work on the wine throughout my childhood."

Foot of the Class

"I went to a one room school that had the first to the sixth grade. There were three or four students in each grade. When lessons were heard, the students were called up to the teacher's desk and asked to recite the lesson of the day. The seating was arranged according to how you stood in class. The ones who had the best grades stood at the head of the class and the ones who had the worst grades stood at the foot of the class.

"When I was in first grade, my father would ask, 'Where did you stand in the class today?' I would say at the foot. Day after day he would ask the same question. Finally I got tired of it and I said, 'Well it could be worse.' He asked, 'How could it be worse? You're already at the foot of the class.' I answered, 'We could have more in the class.' "

Life on the Farm

"I continued to go to the local schools, three different ones in all. One was Retreat Grove, another was Mount Pleasant and the third was Walkersville, where I was born. In Walkersville, I used to stay with my aunt and uncle who lived in town. I stayed with them all week and then went back to the farm on weekends.

"I lived a regular farm life. I hunted rabbits and trapped muskrats and skunks. We'd eat the rabbits. We stretched the muskrat and skunk skins over shingles and sold the skins to local dealers.

"We had no electricity on the farm. We traveled by horse and buggy.

"At age 12, my father sold the farm. I didn't like farm work. My father always had trouble finding me because every time he found me, he had a job for me to do. So, I spent most of my youthful years on the farm avoiding my father. It became increasingly difficult to hide from him, so I was glad when we moved away.

"I don't remember my father calling me by my given name. Every time he would come into the house, he'd say to my mother 'Where is *that boy*?' I began to be known as 'that boy!' So, in 1918, my father, mother and *that boy*, moved to town, which was four miles away."

Church

"I didn't attend Church regularly. Maybe at Christmas time, I would go. The church would have some kind of a pageant. The kids would participate in the program by getting up and reading verses from the Bible. That's the only time I remember ever being in church.

"My mother and father weren't church people. They were considered good people, but they didn't take time off to go to church. I remember my father saying, 'The cows don't go to church.' There were always chores around the farm. Sunday wasn't any different. We still had to feed the cows and horses, clean out the stables, and all that sort of thing.

"When we moved to town in 1918, I started going to church with a friend. He attended Sunday School and he began to take me with him.

"His family wanted me to join the church. I was going to be confirmed on the Sunday before Easter until the minister discovered that I hadn't been baptized. He took me over to the parsonage and baptized me in the living room. My friend became my God Father. That is how I entered the Methodist Church in 1918."

High School

"In Frederick, the boy's and girl's high schools were separate. There was a tradition that only seniors could go up the front stairs to the school. The school also had elementary grades. I spent some of my elementary years there. The year I became a senior, the town built a new co-ed high school. In this school all the students could go up the front stairs. I waited all those years to have the special privilege of going up the front stairs and my ambition was never realized. That was a disappointment to me.

"I didn't particularly like school. I didn't get very good grades. I was good at basketball and that was about it. Although I played baseball, I didn't really like the game. However, I did enjoy football. In my senior year, the school didn't have enough money to support the team, so we had to supply our own uniforms. Some of the kids used horse pads for shoulder pads, and one fellow took a pair of high-top button shoes to the shoemaker and had cleats put on them. Then we ran out of money and the school abandoned football.

"Our basketball team became state champions. This same team played for five different organizations in town, five nights a week. We just changed uniforms, but it was the same team!

"I never did any homework; I never studied. I had been offered several college basketball scholarships, but I didn't accept any of them, because I didn't think I could pass the entrance exam. So, after graduation, I had no school to go to in the fall."

Electrical Training

"A friend of mine went to Bliss Electrical School, a trade school, in Tacoma Park, Maryland. I went there for one year of training in 1926.

"After this schooling, I didn't have a job. A classmate, with whom I played basketball, had a father who was an alcoholic. He took his father down to Florida to get him straightened out. He came back saying that everything was booming in Florida, and that I wouldn't have any trouble getting a job down there.

"So I went with him to Florida in a Model T Ford Roadster. It took about a week. We moved to a little town called Hollywood. It was named by the guy who had developed Hollywood, California. He came to Florida to do the same thing that he had done in California. But the Hollywood, Florida boom turned into a bust.

"I applied for a job at the Florida Department of Light, but I was told that there were no jobs. We were there about a week, when Florida had one of the worse hurricanes it has ever had.

"The hurricane knocked the town absolutely flat. We ended up living in a little shack, built out of piano boxes and stuff. Since the town was without power, I went back to the Florida Department of Light looking for a job. The company said they didn't have any jobs for a fellow with electrical training, all they had were jobs digging pole holes and stringing power lines. I said I knew how to dig pole holes. I got the job.

"The entire town was devastated. Most of the poles had been blown over, those that weren't we took down ourselves. We wrapped and re-spliced all the lines. Then we put up all new poles and set new meters.

"I progressed from one job to another, from digging pole holes to running wires. All the meters had to be reworked, and since I knew how to test meters, I became the one man meter department. I tested and repaired meters night and day. I ended up working there for a couple of years.

"Then I became involved with a Florida basketball team, called The Miami Basketball Club. I made the team and quit my Florida Department of Light job. I played with the team for two seasons in 1927-1928. Then I went back to Florida and did odd jobs for the summer.

"The stock market crashed in 1929. I came home to Frederick and applied for a job with the local power company. I ended up with a very good job in the engineering department of Potomac Edison Power. I sailed through the depression on a salary of $110 a month. I worked there for the next twelve years, designing and laying out electrical lines."

Marriage

"In 1930, I met my wife, Betty. Her family had sent her to college in Frederick. She was engaged to a hometown boy, but we fell in love and she broke off her engagement. That made me a nobody in the eyes of her mother and father.

"Betty's parents decided not to send her back to school. That meant we wouldn't be able to see each other anymore. So we decided to get married and keep it a secret. We were married on May 30, 1930. But, Betty's mother found out and said there would be no secret marriages in her family. I called my wife Betty, but her mother always called her Elizabeth.

"Our marriage started out very rocky. We were married about a month when I said that I was sorry I ever met her.

My wife said she didn't know that I drank till I came home sober one night. She didn't drink before she married me. This was during Prohibition.

"In 1918, when the men were away fighting the First World War, the women all got together and voted liquor out of the country. Liquor wouldn't be legal again until 1933.

"So, drinking was confined to rotgut liquor or home brew. There were no bars or public places where liquor was served, so we'd go to someone's cellar and have a wild party.

"I got drunk every weekend. My wife would take care of me. One weekend, rather than bringing me home drunk, she left me at a friend's house to sleep it off in the bathtub.

"She got tired of taking care of me and she started drinking herself. We got into some really heavy drinking. Then I met the Oxford Group. That was the thing that completely changed both our lives."

The Oxford Group

"The Oxford Group started out with just men. Many of the wives felt that the Oxford Group took priority over them, so they viewed the Group as the enemy. They wanted their husbands to stay away from the Oxford Group.

"But, eventually more and more women became involved. Betty came into the Oxford Group with me and that is what saved our marriage."

World War Two

"In 1942, when America was just getting into the Second Word War, a friend of mine from the power company had gone to work for a company near Washington, D.C. called Electronics Engineering. He became a purchasing agent. Then, Vince Bendix, the man who invented the automobile starter spring, came to Washington and bought the company for $100,000. He moved the company from Washington to Towson, Maryland and named the new plant Bendix Radio.

"This friend of mine wanted me to become a buyer for the company. I didn't know anything about buying, but he said he'd teach me because they desperately needed someone to purchase electronic parts. At the time, I was making about $130 a month. I said that I wouldn't come to work for less than $300 a month. He said, 'That's peanuts.'

"So, I went to work for Bendix Radio for $300 a month. What I found out later was that whatever you asked for, that's what you got. So, I got $300 a month.

"I became a buyer who knew nothing about buying. After two weeks of training, I was called into the bosses office and told, 'Here's your commodity list, there's your desk, there's your secretary, now you're a buyer.' Within about a week, I had orders coming across my desk for about a million radio tubes at a dollar apiece. I never knew there were that many tubes in the world."

After the War

"After the war, I met a salesman who represented several companies. He worked out of Philadelphia. He offered me a job, selling his product line. We worked together for a couple of years. Then he divided his product lines which put me in business for myself. I called my company J. H. Electronic Sales. I worked about 20 years as a manufacture's representative in Baltimore and Washington. I retired in 1966.

"One day my kids asked me what I did for a living. I told them I was a manufacture's representative. They told me the kids at school said I was just a peddler. I said, 'That's right. A manufacture's representative is just a fancy name for a peddler.' "

Wally
"That should do it, James. I think it's time for you to take a nap so you'll be rested for the memorial service at Dr. Bob's House."

James
"I thought you'd never ask."

With the interview over, James closed his eyes. In a minute or two he was sound asleep, and remained so until we exited the freeway in Akron, Ohio.

Another turning point in my spiritual journey with James Houck came in September of 1999. It was during a trip to Clare Michigan for a *Back to Basics* seminar that James relayed another revolutionary concept to me: "fingertip guidance."

By this time, we had been conducting seminars on two-way prayer for more than two years. Tens of thousands of people had found the spiritual solution they were looking for in the *How to Listen to God* pamphlet and the simple Oxford Group program.

Although James was 93 years old, he was still in good health and great spirits. At the Clare, Michigan seminar, he was scheduled to tell his story at four-thirty in the afternoon, after the completion of the *Back to Basics* program.

As soon as I introduced him at the podium, he headed for the front of the stage. Pacing back and forth, he took us back to the early days of the Oxford Group and told us how two-way prayer had changed his life.

After spending forty-five minutes describing his spiritual journey, he walked back to the podium and closed with a call to action:

"I am reminded of a professor of religion at Yale University by the name of Henry Wright. He had inscribed on a wall of his classroom these words":

> **"The world has yet to see what can be accom-**
> **plished by, with, and through one person totally**
> **committed to doing the will of God."**

"Then, he would ask his students this question, and I ask it again this afternoon":

> **"Will you be that person?"**

After James issued this challenge, there was not a sound in the room for at least ten seconds. Then one person shouted, "yes" followed by another and another. A few people started clapping and in a few seconds, the applause turned into a thunderous standing ovation.

James spent the next hour working one-on-one with those who stayed after the meeting to learn more about the basics of two-way prayer and life-changing from this spiritually connected "elder of the tribe."

James had received this title from Jimmy, a native American from the Chippewa tribe who had his life changed by the *How to Listen to God* pamphlet about a year before. When he started listening, he was guided to meet James and video tape him for a documentary.

During our seminar at the Wilson House in April 1999, Jimmy spent four days with James and the *Back to Basics* team. He shot more than twenty hours of video tape. When I asked him why he had put much time into recording James, he answered, "Don't you realize who this man is?" "He's a spiritual giant who has saved more than one hundred thousand lives," I replied. Jimmy responded, "In my culture he's even more important than that. He is the 'elder of the tribe.' 'He's everybody's grandfather.' "

Following the seminar, James and I spent a few more days in Michigan continuing our life-changing efforts. Then it was time to return home.

Charlie volunteered to drive us to the airport which was two hours away. We put James in the back seat and I settled into the front passenger's seat.

We spent the first half hour in general conversation about the seminar and continuing to share guidance with those who had already had their lives changed. These people would become the core of the Clare, Michigan team.

Then James asked Charlie, "What about your guidance today? What is God's plan for you?" Charlie hesitatingly replied, "James, I'm still having a problem with guidance. I listen, but the thoughts come so quickly I can't write them down fast enough."

James thought about this for a moment, then said, "Charlie, from time to time we all have difficulty getting the words on paper, for whatever reason. When this happens, we usually try 'fingertip guidance.' "

James' words immediately captured my attention. He had not talked about this before. What was "fingertip guidance," I asked?

James told us the story of how "fingertip guidance" came about in the 1930's when an Oxford Group team was in South Africa trying to solve racial problems through the use of two-way prayer. Upon their arrival, the team encountered a black population that could speak English but, because of the lack of education, could not read or write English.

Faced with this dilemma, the team came up with "fingertip guidance." This is how it works:

1.   Get quiet.

2.   Invite God into your life.

3.   Listen.

4.   As soon as a thought comes into your mind, touch your thumb to your first finger to capture it.

5.   When another thought comes, capture it by touching your thumb to your second finger.

6.   Keep recording until you either run out of thoughts or fingers.

After describing the process, James explained the significance of "fingertip guidance." "Even if you can only capture one or two thoughts, it's far better than letting all of them slip away. What do you think, Charlie? Are you ready to give it a try?"

Charlie was hesitant, but he did let James know he was willing to proceed.

James continued, "Charlie, you said you did a 'quiet time' this morning, but the thoughts came so fast you couldn't get them on paper."

"That's right. They got away before I could record them."

"Well, let's see what you might have captured, without even knowing it. Touch your thumb to your first finger. What do you hear?"

"Call Joe."

"Ok, touch your thumb to your second finger. Now, what do you hear?"

"Take Mom to see the foliage."

"Good. How about the third finger?"

"Nothing."

"And the fourth finger?"

"Nothing."

Then James checked to make sure Charlie's guidance wasn't for somebody else. "Wally, does, 'Call Joe' mean anything to you?"

"Nothing comes to mind," I answered.

"Me either. I think this guidance is for you, Charlie. So what does 'Call Joe' mean?"

Charlie thought about it for a moment and replied, "I don't know any Joe–I can't even think of a Joe to call."

James pressed on. "This is very interesting. Maybe we all need to listen so God can tell us what 'Call Joe' means. Let's take a 'quiet time' and ask God for additional information about Joe and why we're supposed to call him."

We all sat quietly and waited for guidance. My mind was racing. What was this all about? I had never witnessed anything like this before.

After about three minutes, Charlie exclaimed, "Oh, my God. I do know a Joe."

James smiled. He asked Charlie to explain what had just come to him.

"Several years ago I went to meetings with a guy named Joe. He stuck around for a while, got bored and left. Last night, as I was driving by the one of the local bars, I remember seeing his truck in the parking lot."

James responded, "Charlie, this sure sounds like guidance to me. Why don't you give this Joe a call? Maybe he needs your help."

I was awestruck by the simplicity of the process and the possibility that two words captured on a fingertip could save a life. I knew this was a guidance session I would never forget.

About a week later, I called Charlie from Tucson. I was curious as to what had happened.

Charlie told me he had second thoughts about what had taken place in the car. As soon as he dropped us off at the airport, he began to doubt the validity of the experience. His mind kept telling him this could not be guidance–it was just a figment of his imagination.

I asked Charlie if he had followed up on the second piece of "fingertip guidance." He said he had. Over the weekend, he had taken his invalid mother for a four-hour drive through the countryside to see the autumn colors. He said it was easy to follow this guidance because it was something he had already planned to do. This business about calling Joe was different. There was no reason for that thought to be in his head.

I agreed. That is why it was so important to find out where this guidance had come from. I did not know if Charlie's "fingertip guidance" was real or not, but as far as I was concerned, it did pass the test of Honesty, Purity, Unselfishness and Love, whereas his later thoughts did not. As I saw it, self was trying to disconnect him from the Voice within. I concluded by saying, "The only way you'll know for sure whose voice you heard is to follow through on the guidance." Charlie promised me he would make the call.

I waited another week and telephoned Charlie back. When Charlie opened the conversation with, "Wally, you're not going to believe this," I knew that, not only was I going to believe it, I was going to grow from listening to Charlie's experience.

"The day after we talked, I called Joe. He was in terrible shape. He was on the verge of drinking himself to death. I made a few phone calls and got him into a detox."

Charlie was awestruck by what had happened. He said, "James is a miracle worker. But, how did he know?"

"I would imagine he didn't," I replied. "James just provided us with a simple technique we could use to make contact with God. After that, God did the rest.

"You may have been the only person Joe would have

listened to. God knew that. That's why God put the thought on your fingertip to contact him. There's no telling what would have happened if you hadn't called Joe, but under the circumstances, I don't think it would have been very pleasant.

"God provided the directions and who knows, you just might have changed a life. From the way you're talking, I think God changed your life in the process. I know that "fingertip guidance" has certainly changed mine."

Since this turning point in central Michigan, I have made "fingertip guidance" an integral part of my *How to Listen to God* presentations. I have now witnessed many miracles just like the one that happened to Charlie. "It works–it really does!"

4
Putting the Pieces Together

James Houck makes public speaking look easy. Even though he has had no formal training and only limited experience prior to 1996, he has quickly become a master at capturing and holding an audience's attention. During the past four years, I have watched James change tens of thousands of lives just by telling his story and explaining, from first hand experience, the simple Four Step program of two-way prayer.

James' contribution to the spiritual community in general and the recovering community in particular is unprecedented. Without James, there would be no *Back to Basics* program for those who wish to recover from addictive behaviors, or the *Converting Barriers to Bridges* program for those in need of a spiritual solution to any and all of life's difficulties. Both programs use the *How to Listen to God* pamphlet as the foundation for the transformation from a self-directed to a God directed life.

Watching James at work is a spiritual experience in itself. It is almost beyond comprehension that a man in his nineties could be so mentally alert, physically agile, and spiritually alive. Although his short term memory fails at times, he can describe events from the 1930's and 1940's as if they happened yesterday.

James does not like being confined to a podium, so he requests a wireless lapel microphone whenever he speaks. He says he needs the mobility so he can reach out to everyone in the audience.

He delivers one of the greatest messages of hope ever recorded. Because of his passion for two-way prayer and life-changing, he is graciously received everywhere he speaks.

As the elder statesman for the Oxford Group program of the 1930's and the Twelve Step Movement of the 1940's, James is audio taped at every speaking engagement. On occasion, he is videotaped as well. These recordings are for those who will not have the opportunity to meet James in person.

Although James and I have been co-presenters at numerous events throughout the United States during the past four years, I will use James' first presentation at a *Back to Basics* conference as an example of his magnetism and universal appeal.

On Friday, November 11, 1997, James Houck changed the course of history. This was the first time anyone, including James, realized that the *Back to Basics* program could bring large numbers of people to a new awareness of God and their place in God's universe.

The meeting was held at the Obregon Methodist Church in Dayton, Ohio. Ronnie, our host and meeting coordinator, was unsure how many people would attend because we were resurrecting a historically accurate though long forgotten message.

James was to speak at eight o'clock. The weather was cold–below freezing with snow flurries. We arrived at seven thirty thinking we would be ahead of the crowd, if there was to be one. Not only was the church parking lot full but some of Ronnie's friends were already directing traffic to other lots located several blocks away.

After dropping James off at the front door, I parked the rental car and made my way through the crowd, video equipment in hand. The meeting room was packed to over-flowing. All the chairs were taken and people were sitting in the aisles and standing against the walls. They were also standing in an adjoining room and in the hallway.

I asked several people in the center aisle to move closer together so I could set up the camera tripod. I mounted the camera and connected it to an extension cord the audio taper had provided. Because there was no place to sit, I crawled under the tripod.

As I was getting settled in, the meeting began. I hit the record button and sat back down to watch. Ronnie was the first to speak.

Ronnie

"Wow! There must be six hundred people here tonight. Since there are only two hundred fifty chairs in this room, I don't know how we all got in here, but I'm glad we did.

"As you know, some people didn't want this *Back to Basics* weekend to happen. But based on this turnout, it's obvious that God had a different plan.

"When I left the office yesterday, I told my co-workers I probably wouldn't get much sleep last night and, sure enough, I was so excited, I only slept about an hour and a half. Yet, I'm still going strong. I probably won't get much sleep tonight, either.

"I am elated to be in the midst of something this awesome–something that will probably only happen once in my lifetime. Several months ago, I started talking to Wally about *Back to Basics*, and he told me about James Houck. I had no idea there was anyone left alive who was around when the Twelve Step Movement started. I was amazed to learn that James knew Bill Wilson and had gone to meetings with him years before the 'Big Book' was written.

"James has almost 63 years of sobriety. The original Twelve Step program just celebrated its sixty-second anniversary this past June. James has been sober longer than the Twelve Step Movement has been in existence. (Applause) Let's give him a warm Dayton welcome–James Houck." (Thunderous applause followed by a standing ovation.)

James Houck

"I haven't even said anything yet. (Laughter) This crowd here tonight really amazes me.

"Thank you, Ronnie. I feel like a mosquito in a nudist colony–I just don't know where to begin. (Laughter)

"I think I will start by saying that I am a friend of Bill Wilson. A lot of people can say they knew Bill Wilson, but I was a friend of Bill Wilson back in 1935. Some people are amazed by that and they ask, 'How in the world did you ever know Bill Wilson?' Well, you have to be very old to have known Bill Wilson back then. (Laughter) You see, in February I'll be ninety-two years old.

"Before we get started tonight, I need to make a special announcement. I was just handed a piece of paper that says there is a person here tonight who has traveled two hundred miles for this meeting and this person is **111** years old. Now, will that person please stand so we can welcome you? (No response–some members of the audience start looking around.) If you can't stand, maybe you could just raise your hand. (No response–now everyone is looking around.)

"Maybe there's a name on this note? (Pause) I'm sorry, we seem to be getting off on the wrong foot here. I have really goofed. This note doesn't say this person is **111** years old, it says they are **ill**. (Loud laughter) That's the reason they're not at the meeting tonight. I wondered about that.

"However, I did have an aunt who lived to be one hundred and two. She never used glasses–she drank right out of the bottle the whole time. (Laughter)

"A few years ago a company tried to put a retirement plan into place. In order for this plan to be effective every employee in the company had to sign up for it. There was a man by the name of Joe who said he didn't understand the plan and therefore wasn't going to sign up.

"The other employees became anxious, so they worked on Joe. The foreman, the department head, even the vice president, tried to get Joe to sign up for the plan. But, Joe insisted that he wasn't going to sign.

"Finally, the president got involved. He said, 'Send Joe up to me, I want to talk to him.' When Joe arrived in his office, the president said, 'Joe, they tell me you won't sign up for the plan.' 'That's right,' Joe replied. 'I never sign anything I don't understand.'

The president then told Joe, 'Let me explain it to you this way, either you sign up for the plan or you're fired.' So, Joe took the plan, looked it over, signed it and handed it back. The president asked, 'Why didn't you do that in the first place.' Joe answered, 'No one ever explained it to me like that before.' (Laughter)

"I tell this story because I hope that everyone here tonight will go away from this meeting saying the same thing–no one ever explained the Twelve Step Movement and the Oxford Group like that before.

"Right off the bat, I want to tell you I'm not what some folks call a California comedian or an entertainer. I am not a professional speaker. With my voice, I would have been run off the first platform I ever stood on. But, I do know certain facts–certain truths that I would like to share with you. I do believe this knowledge qualifies me to be here.

"Tonight, I'm going to explain to you what it was like back when I knew Bill Wilson. As I said, that was a long, long time ago. But, before I do, I'd like to tell you a little bit about myself. Then I will tell you about Bill Wilson.

"I had my first drink when I was five years old. I used to get into my mother's dandelion wine. I would then fill the bottles with water so she wouldn't know some of the wine was missing. Of course, I know that none of you have done anything like that.

"When I was six years old, I started school. On the first day of class, I took a pint of dandelion wine with me. I was drinking it like it was Coca-Cola. I didn't know the difference. I was very disappointed when my teacher took it away from me. (Laughter)

"I drank all during school. After high school, I stormed around the country for a number of years with a traveling basketball team. I played in the National Amateur Championships for a couple of years.

"After that, I worked for a power company–actually several power companies. In 1930 I met and married a woman named Betty. I was 24 years old at the time. Betty had come to Frederick, Maryland to go to school. Frederick is a small community west of Baltimore, where I was living. She had only known me nine months when I talked her into running off and getting married.

"Her parents had already checked me out. They had gotten a bad report from one of the town fathers who said I had never worked a day in my life. So, Betty's parents told her I wasn't any good to start with. But, she married me anyway.

"I wasn't married a month before I told her I was sorry I ever met her. I wasn't used to being tied down. Until then, I had been a free agent–running the range.

"Betty was a very proud girl. She wasn't about to go home and tell her parents that they were right–that I wasn't any good. So she decided to stick it out. So here we were four and a half years later in the middle of an armed truce marriage going nowhere but downhill.

"It was then that I met the Oxford Group. Several months later, I met Bill Wilson.

"First, I want to tell you that when I met the Oxford Group there wasn't any such thing as the Twelve Step Movement. I know this may be difficult for some people to understand, but Bill Wilson, Dr. Bob, the other Twelve Step pioneers were all in the Oxford Group. We all got sober taking the Oxford Group Four Steps, not the Twelve Steps. Almost everything in the Twelve Step program came directly from the Oxford Group. The Oxford Group provided all the source material.

"I met the Oxford Group on Dec. 12, 1934 at the YMCA in Frederick. I didn't know anything about the organization at the time, but I later learned the Oxford Group was basically a one-on-one, evangelistic movement. The leader was a man by the name of Frank Buchman, a Pennsylvania born, Lutheran minister.

"His idea was to take people to a new level in terms of their relationship with God. He was not interested in converting people as such. He didn't try to bring people into a movement. Rather, he tried to put movement into people.

"Buchman would say there are many things that will make a person good. But, in many cases they end up being good for nothing, because they don't have any purpose for their lives. That is what the Oxford Group provided–a new way of living with purpose and direction.

"Buchman brought three things to the Oxford Group. The first one was the Four Standards of Honesty, Purity,

Unselfishness and Love. These were taken from the Sermon on the Mount. In 1902, Robert Speer, a Presbyterian theologian took the fifth, sixth and seventh chapters of Matthew and boiled the message down to its essence. He said that Christ's words could be summarized into these four categories.

"The second thing Buchman brought to the Oxford Group was two-way prayer: talking to God and listening to God. He said that almost everyone prays to God through their mind. They usually don't pray out loud. They talk to God through their thoughts. That seems logical. Well if it's logical to believe we talk to God through our mind, isn't it just as logical that God is going to talk to us the same way, through our thoughts. This made sense to me.

"The third thing was restitution, which is putting right the things that are wrong. In the Twelve Step Movement we call this making amends. All three of these principles have been incorporated into the Twelve Step programs. Bill gave us the opposites of the Four Standards in the Fourth, Tenth and Eleventh Steps. Restitution is Steps Eight and Nine. Two-way prayer is Step Eleven.

"These are the three things that became the basis of the Oxford Group program: the Four Standards, listening to God, and Restitution. I'll tell you more about Restitution in a moment.

"As I sat in that YMCA meeting room listening to all this, I wasn't convinced that God could speak to me. So, they said, 'Why don't you experiment with it?' It was a dare of sorts. Finally I said, 'Okay, I take your dare.'

"So, I got quiet and opened up my mind to God. The very

first thought that came to me was to go back and straighten out some damage I had caused five years earlier when I wrecked a car while driving drunk.

"I was working for an electric company out in New York, but we had access to cars from the local power company. One weekend, I took a car out to go to a University of Maryland football game. I got drunk, ran into a parked car and didn't stop. I thought no one had gotten my license, but someone had.

"I took the car home and fixed it up. I even took the extra precaution of paying the fellow at the garage to say I didn't have the car out. The police came to investigate and, sure enough, my story held up. The police went away and the matter was dropped.

"Now, in the five years since this happened, I had never given it another thought. For that event to come into my mind the first time I practiced 'quiet time' wasn't humanly possible. There had to be something supernatural at work here. So that first guidance session started to make a believer out of me.

"Later on during that meeting at the YMCA, I sat down with a man and we talked about our lives. He told me about an incident in his life that was bothering him. Then, he asked me to describe the things I had done that I felt ashamed of. I talked about my anger and my guilt. He told me he had these same feelings but had gotten rid of them by turning them over to God and making restitution. He asked me if I was ready to do the same. When I told him I was, we said a little prayer together.

"Now if you follow closely what I am describing here, you'll see that I am talking about the Twelve Step program. Maybe some of us haven't done all these things. We haven't gotten beyond the alcohol part. We haven't done those things which take us beyond alcohol to a new way of living. We think that it's all about not drinking when it is much more than that. It's about eliminating those things that have cut us off from God so we can follow God's plan for our lives.

"So, let's think about these things as we go along, because what I am describing is the original program. This is what Bill Wilson did and this is what Dr. Bob did.

"After this meeting at the YMCA, I began each day by listening to God. How many here tonight have morning devotions? (Hundreds of hands go up.) Most of you are familiar with this. So, I began having a morning devotion, and God began putting thoughts into my mind that I had never had before.

"As I told you, I worked for a power company. I was paid a salary but I also worked overtime. I didn't get paid for overtime, so I had no qualms about padding my expense account. I felt they owed me the money and this was the way to get it. I also threw my personal mail in with the company mail. This way I sent all my letters for free.

"But worst of all, I had a jumper on my electric meter. In the eyes of a power company, the lowest form of humanity was a guy with a jumper on his electric meter. I not only had a jumper on my meter, I also had a jumper on my mother's meter. She owned a restaurant, so that would have been a big bill.

"During one of my 'quiet times,' I received guidance to make restitution for the jumpers on the meters. I always thought restitution meant cleaning your own slate and making a nice fresh start–all that sort of thing. Yes, it's that, but it's much more. The big thing is what it does for the other fellow.

"I went to my boss and told him I had been stealing from the company. He was shocked. Nobody had ever come clean like this before. He said, 'Jim, I don't know how to handle this. What do you want me to do?' I answered, 'I don't know, I just want to pay the money back.' Finally he got an idea. He told me to go see Wilson Cook.

Now, Wilson Cook's job–his only job–was to convince customers that their electric bills were not too high. People were constantly coming in and complaining that their electric meter was running too fast. Well, I had worked in the meter department and I knew that it was impossible to make a meter run more than 10 percent above design. So, we're not talking about much money, but, nonetheless, it was Wilson Cook's job to persuade the customers their bills were correct. In other words, he spent all day convincing people to pay more than they thought they should.

"Wilson didn't know what to think when I breezed into his office and told him I was stealing from the company. He was even more confused when I told him I wanted to pay it back. He said, 'How much do you think you owe?' I told him that, according to my figures, it must be around five hundred dollars. Now, that was a lot of money in the 1930's especially during the depression. I only made one hundred twenty-five dollars per month, so this was almost four month's salary.

"Wilson's first remark was, 'Oh, it couldn't be that much.' (Laughter) He proceeded to talk me down to two hundred fifty dollars. So this was a man who earned his living convincing people to pay more and here he was trying to talk me into paying less.

"Then Wilson asked me how I wanted to pay the bill. I told him that was going to be difficult because I didn't have any money. (Laughter) So Wilson and I made an arrangement where I paid so much each payday. Wilson collected money from me for the next two years. But, at least I didn't get fired which is what probably would have happened if I hadn't been honest and they'd found out about the jumpers on their own.

"Then I began to get other thoughts during my morning 'quiet time.' In 1918, when I was 12 years old, our family moved from the farm to the city. It was the first time we had electric lights. I was fascinated with this idea of electricity because on the farm all we had were kerosene lamps. I thought about running extensions to light the entire house.

"I got a job working for a man who owned an electric store. I worked for a nickel an hour. I worked ten hours a day, six days a week for three bucks a week.

"On three bucks a week I couldn't buy extensions, so I stole them. I made deliveries and, from time to time, I would wrap up an extra extension and carry it out of the store.

"It is now sixteen years later and God is telling me to go back and make restitution to this store owner. I didn't know how much money I owed, but I knew I had to repay it. Well, things were a little sticky because this guy and I were on the same Methodist Church board.

"I got up the courage and went to see him. I told him I had stolen from him sixteen years before and I offered him some money. He was amazed. He said, 'I can't take this money. I'll have to give it to the church or something.' I said, 'Well that's your problem, my guidance is to give the money to you.'

"Then he said something that I thought was very strange. He asked me if I had time for coffee. I said, 'yes,' so we went across the street.

"When we were sitting down at the restaurant, he said, 'Look Jim, I've never had anyone be dead honest with me the way you were. I want you to know that it touched me very deeply. Because of what you have just shared with me, I feel I need to share something with you.'

"My wife and I are on the verge of divorce. I haven't been faithful to her, the papers are drawn and I don't see any way out. But, what you just did has given me a completely new idea. I am going to go home and be as honest with her about my life as you have been with me about yours. I'm going to see if we can straighten this mess out.' This he did. As a direct result of his honesty, he was able to save his marriage.

"I began to see the power of this thing called restitution. Here I was only about two or three weeks into the Oxford Group program, and I was already witnessing lives being changed. This affected me greatly. By being honest with another person, not only was my life changed, but so was another person's.

"I found my drinking problem had disappeared. I kept thinking about how God had used me to change a man's life. I began to see what Buchman meant when he talked about using restitution to become a life-changer.

"Now, I could have gone to this fellow and said, 'Look Homer, it's being rumored all over town that you're running around. Why don't you straighten up and fly right?' Well, he probably would have told me to go to hell, and rightly so. But,

I simply went to him and shared the deepest thing in my heart because this is what God had told me to do. By following guidance, I helped save a couple's marriage. That, to me, was an amazing thing.

"My next guidance was to straighten things out with my wife. It took me three nights to tell her all the things that were on my mind. She had no idea what kind of person I really was. Prior to our marriage, she had only known me for nine months, and that was on weekends. Since she couldn't leave school at night, she knew very little about my carousing and running around during the week.

"Years before, I'd told her I wished I'd never met her. But, because of her pride, she had decided to stick it out. Since she wanted the marriage to work, I told her it was for the best that she knew these things about me.

"I talked to Betty when I came home from work, through the dinner hour, and until we went to bed. It took three nights to tell her all of the things that she needed to know about me. I didn't hold anything back. I was just dead honest with her about everything.

"At the time, my sister was making book that my marriage would not last a year. And, a marriage that wasn't supposed to last a year lasted fifty-seven years as the direct result of practicing 'quiet time and guidance.' (Applause)

"I started going to Oxford Group meetings on Saturday night in Frederick at the Francis Scott Key Hotel. One Saturday, when I was leading the meeting, a tall, thin fellow came in. He said his name was Bill Wilson and that he lived in New York City. He introduced me to a friend of his but I don't remember too much about him. I do remember Bill, because the next thing he said was, 'Are you going to have any drunks here tonight?' I answered, 'Well Bill, we don't single the drunks out.' Bill then said, 'If you have any drunks, send them my way.'

"I know this is hard for many in the Twelve Step Movement to understand. The Oxford Group never made alcohol a separate issue. To the Group, alcohol wasn't any different from smoking or womanizing. They were all on the same level–they all cut you off from God.

"In the Oxford Group, we dealt with sin in people's lives. We don't hear this word used much anymore. In the Group, we were told that sin was anything that separated us from God or from other people. John Wesley, the Methodist theologian, used to say that whenever your body takes authority over your mind, that was sin no matter how innocent it may seem. This definition covers all addictions and obsessions. So, smoking, drinking and womanizing are all considered to be sins.

"I attended Oxford Group meetings with Bill in Frederick from 1935 until 1937. In the summer, he was at the meetings several times a month, in the winter about every four to six weeks.

"During this time, Bill also attended meetings in New York City at the Calvary Church. It was at these meetings that Bill became a good friend of Sam Shoemaker.

"In 1937, I started traveling to New York on weekends to meet with Sam and, from time to time, I would run into Bill. During this time, I got to know most of the New York City team.

"This went on until the fall of 1937 when Bill decided to leave the Oxford Group. Bill went to Frank Buchman and told him he felt that he should give full time to alcoholics.

"Frank listened and then said, 'Bill, if that is the biggest thing you see for yourself, go for it. But, keep in mind we're dealing with alcoholic nations rather than just alcoholic people.' Frank was trying to tell Bill the Oxford Group would continue to deal with all problems, not just alcohol.

"It was at this time that I lost touch with Bill. I didn't see much of him after that.

"Some people think that when Bill left the Oxford Group, he took all the drunks with him. That wasn't the case. Rowland Hazard, Charles Clapp, Victor Kitchen and I, among others, stayed behind. By then we were busy trying to change the world. Besides, many of us thought Bill pulled out of the Oxford Group because he didn't want anyone checking up on his smoking and womanizing.

"So, Bill left the Oxford Group to concentrate on alcoholics. Most of you know the story after that. He took the Oxford Group Four Steps and converted them into the Twelve Step program. In 1939, he wrote a book to help alcoholics find God.

"In 1935, when Bill got started, he worked with about fifty alcoholics in his first six months. At the end of that time, not one of them was any different. He was going to quit, but his wife Lois told him, 'Look Bill, you've got to remember that not once during this time, did you want to drink.' From her comment, Bill realized the value of helping others. It didn't matter whether or not they got it, he had to keep trying.

"So, the necessity of working with others became the heart of the Twelve Step Movement, just as it had been in the Oxford Group. It is just as important today as it was back then. I don't know why, but for some reason, we don't seem to apply this principle the way we used to in the early days.

"Dr. Bob, Bill and the other early members would go any place, any time, day or night to a jail, flop house, or street corner to help a drunk who was in trouble. But I don't see this happening now. That's one of the things that I'm going to talk about tonight. How do we get back to the spiritual roots of the original program? How do we get back to the basics?

"The Twelve Step Movement is not about not drinking. It's about finding God and having God take care of all of our problems. Alcohol is only mentioned once–in the first step. The rest of the steps have to do with finding God.

"For instance, in the Fourth Step, Bill talks about taking a fearless moral inventory. He also asks us to test our actions to see if they are God directed or self-directed.

"Then he asks us to turn those things that are self-directed over to God. Aren't we supposed to ask God to remove everything that separates us from Him and our fellows? Then why would we only turn over alcohol and not the other things that have us blocked off from God.

"Let's see, where were we? Bill left the Oxford Group in 1937 and he began to write the 'Big Book.' Dr. Bob and the Akron team helped him write it. Dr. Bob didn't leave the Oxford Group until after the book was written.

"Let me say a word about Akron. Dr. Bob was the spiritual

powerhouse of the Twelve Step program. Although I didn't know Dr. Bob, I did know T. Henry Williams, who hosted the Oxford Group meeting in Akron and Henrietta Seiberling, the lady who brought Bill and Dr. Bob together.

"T. Henry was a mechanical engineer who invented the molds for retreading tires. Now back in the 1930's re-treading tires was a big thing. Because he developed these molds, he was in touch with Firestone, Goodyear, Ford and the other automobile people in the area.

"Harvey Firestone's son, Bud, was the Akron town drunk. In 1931, the Oxford Group changed his life. On a train from Denver to Chicago, Bud made a decision to surrender his life to God. Sam Shoemaker and another man took him through the Steps and he had a conversion experience. Bud stopped drinking and became an active member of the Oxford Group.

"Then in 1933, Harvey Firestone and Rev. Walter Tunks invited an Oxford Group team to Akron for a week. Harvey Firestone was 'ace high' on the Oxford Group for saving his son's life.

"Frank Buchman was there. The Oxford Group held meetings all over town, including the Mayflower hotel. Henrietta Seiberling and Anne Smith, Dr. Bob's wife, were at those meetings. Later they talked Dr. Bob into attending the meetings that started up at T. Henry and Clarace Williams' house.

"I'm sure most of you know the story of the Mayflower Hotel. In 1935, Bill went to Akron on a business deal that went bust leaving him stranded at the Mayflower. He started calling around looking for someone in the Oxford Group. He called

Reverend Tunks who gave him the name of Henrietta Seiberling. Henrietta introduced Bill to Dr. Bob the next day.

"Henrietta had been praying for an answer for Dr. Bob. Even though he was in the Oxford Group, Dr. Bob was still drinking. A couple of weeks before this, Henrietta had called the Akron team together to try to help Dr. Bob. She shared her guidance which was to bring something new into Dr. Bob's life. She asked everyone to come to the meeting ready to share something from their lives they had never shared before. Henrietta hoped this would bring a new spiritual element into the meeting.

"That's exactly what happened. Everyone made a confession and this triggered something in Dr. Bob. He told everyone he was a secret drinker. Then they all got together and prayed. This surrender changed Dr. Bob's life.

"That is the reason T. Henry Williams would point to a spot on his living room floor and say, 'This is where (the Twelve Step Movement) started–right here, when Dr. Bob gave his life to God.' But, Henrietta Seiberling would disagree. She'd say, 'No, it started at my house when Bill and Dr. Bob first met.' Regardless it started in Akron. There is no question about that.

"You see, Bill was an atheist before he met the Oxford Group. Sometimes, when I mention this, someone will say, 'Really? I didn't think Bill had any religion at all.' (Laughter)

"Many of you have read the account of how, in Towns Hospital, Bill had this strange feeling come over him. Then, his hospital room lit up like a thousand watt bulb.

"But, Bill saw the Oxford Group differently than Dr. Bob

did. Bill used the Oxford Group like an auto repair shop. He equated alcohol to changing the oil. As far as Bill was concerned, all you had to do was bring your car in regularly to get your oil changed. Bill didn't care if the tires were bad or if the front end was out of alignment or that you had no headlights. As long as the oil was changed, you were okay. Bill was absolutely obsessed with this idea of getting your oil changed, whereas the Oxford Group takes care of the entire car.

"I want to talk to you a little bit tonight about the spiritual side of the Oxford Group. I don't know exactly how to compare it, but as far as I am concerned, it was head and shoulders above any other spiritual movement at the time. This was because the Group dealt with every aspect of a person's life.

"Buchman was not an evangelist as such. He was just interested in getting people changed. He was tremendously interested in getting them to use that change to build a new world. And, he never departed from that philosophy. He said everyone wants to see the other fellow different. Every nation wants to see the other nation different. But everyone and every nation is waiting for the other to begin. He said if you want an answer to the problems of the world, the best place to start is with you.

"That's exactly what Buchman did. He started with the individual. Buchman said, 'You can't make a good omelette out of bad eggs.' He also said, 'You can vote the Democrats in and the Republicans out and then turn around and vote the Republicans in and the Democrats out, but unless you deal with the motives of the people involved you'll always end up with the same thing.' That's what we have today. It doesn't matter whom you vote for if all you get are selfish people concerned with only money and power. Politicians will always be selfish people operating with selfish motives if they don't listen to God. Buchman strongly recommended that everyone use the concepts of two-way prayer and guidance in their lives.

"That is what the *Back to Basics* workshop tomorrow is all about. Wally will take you through the Steps so you can establish a clear channel and start listening to God. It's not a big deal. Anyone can listen to God anywhere, anytime.

"In our meetings, we talk a lot about getting out of self-will and finding God's will for our lives, but very few of us know exactly how to do it. During tomorrow's sessions we're going to learn how to listen to God, how to separate self-thoughts from God thoughts, and how to work with others. Isn't that right, Wally? We're going to learn how to do it all, and it's not that complicated.

"I could go on and tell you many more things about the original program, but tomorrow you'll have the chance to experience it first hand. So, let's take a minute to review what I have just said tonight. In essence, I told you how I took the Oxford Group Four Steps in 1934. You might not have been conscious of it, but we've actually gone through the entire program. I told you I was powerless over alcohol, selfishness and dishonesty. The Oxford Group convinced me that God could solve my problems. Then, I turned my life over to this Power. This was my Surrender.

"I sat down and talked over my life with another person. Until that time, I thought my problems were peculiar to me and no one else had them. But, here was a guy who told me he had the same difficulties, except that God had taken these things out of his life. Then he asked if I was ready to have God take these difficulties away from me. When I told him I was, we said a little prayer asking God to remove alcohol, selfishness and dishonesty from my life. This was Sharing.

"During my 'quiet time,' I kept receiving thoughts about making an amends for the harm I had caused. I tried to set each matter straight to the best of my ability. This was Restitution.

I listen to God every morning, write down what I hear, and act on those thoughts that pass the test of Honesty, Purity, Unselfishness and Love. I check my guidance at night to see if I have followed God's plan for the day. Each day I try to help someone else. This is Guidance which we practice daily for the rest of our lives.

So, tonight we went through all the Steps. This is the way we should go through them, quickly and completely, without even realizing what we've done. When we do this, our lives change because we're now listening to and relying on God to solve all our problems.

"This is exactly what *Back to Basics* is all about. It's a one-on-one life-changing movement. But many of us have not had our lives changed. We've not felt the release that comes from completing the Steps. For us, it's like going to church and never getting beyond the point of our own conversion. There's nothing wrong with it, it's good as far as it goes. But it doesn't result in a spiritual transformation that becomes multiplied into the lives of other people.

"We're guilty of this in the Twelve Step Movement also. We never get beyond our own sobriety. We think it's all about not drinking. We are unable to multiply our spiritual experience into the lives of others.

"Now when I say I have sixty two years of sobriety and that I knew Bill Wilson, people think I can walk on water or something. I tell them, 'Look, sixty two years and a dollar will get you a cup of coffee if the only thing I've done with my life is stay sober.' The important thing is what my life has meant to other people during this time.

"Now, a lot of people get saved in the churches, and its like getting a ticket to heaven. You sit in the station and wait for the heavenly express to take you to the promised land. But what happens to your life while you are waiting in the station? Absolutely nothing.

"You can be good, but if you don't change someone else's life in the process, you can end up being good for nothing. The Oxford Group gave me a purpose for my life, and if you listen to the deepest thing in your heart when you are having 'quiet time,' God will give you a purpose for you life, too.

"Now, let me tell you something about converting barriers to bridges. I don't think there is anyone here tonight who hasn't, at one time or another, said something that you have regretted. Then you go back to that person and apologize. You say, 'I'm sorry. I didn't really mean what I said the other day. I hope you will forgive me.' Invariably, the other person will say, 'Look, it wasn't all your fault. I had a part in it, too.'

"You may not be able to explain it, but what has developed is a new relationship between you and the other person. Something that was a vertical barrier between the two of you has now become a horizontal bridge. Fellowship flows back and forth in a whole new way. This is probably the simplest form of restitution I can think of. It has happened to every one of us. What we need to do is take this idea of converting barriers into bridges and multiply it. We need to ask ourselves, 'How many people have I gotten closer to today?'

"We need to concentrate on helping others by sharing our lives with them. When we're willing to tell someone about an event we are deeply ashamed of–an incident we may have been trying to hide–we bring something new into the life of the other person. If we want to help someone else, we have to be honest about our own life. It is our honesty that touches and changes other people.

"So, why should we continually fight the problem? Why don't we instead try to live in the solution? When we live in the solution, there is no problem. We can all go out from here tonight as changed people, reborn children of God, ambassadors to a new world order. We can become new world builders, because that's the only way we're going to get a new world–by building it with changed people.

People talk about building a new world, but what is the world? For us, the world is the people we come in contact with tonight, tomorrow and the next day–the people around us–that is our world. How are we affecting our world? Sometimes the things we do speak so loudly others can't hear a thing we say. They need to see something new in us. They need to see us acting like changed people, relying on God to help us help our fellows.

"I hope you will come back tomorrow so we can talk some more about this–how to live in the solution by listening to God every day. This is the way the Twelve Step Movement started and it is the only way it can continue to exist. If we take God out of our program, we have nothing. (Thunderous applause)

"Yes, I am circling the field. I want to close by reading a letter written by an Oxford Group member during the Second World War. The man died in combat shortly after he wrote the letter. This was his hope for all of us:

> 'Suppose, we as a nation, find again the faith in God our fathers knew. Suppose our homes become again the nation's strength, our schools the centers of true learning and good citizenship, our farms and factories the pattern of unity, integrity and national service. Suppose our statesmen learn again to listen to the Voice of God. Then we shall know once more the greatness of a nation whose strength is in the spirit of her people.'

"And, you are her people.

"Thank you." (Two minute standing ovation)

**James Houck
One of the greatest life-changers of the
Twentieth Century**

Upper: James and Wally with hosts and co-presenter at a spiritual workshop in Gary, Indiana (June 2000)

Lower: James Houck and co-presenter explaining the Five C's of Life Changing at the Gary, Indiana spiritual workshop (June 2000)

5
God Speaks!

It is time to examine the program as practiced by James Houck and the hundreds of thousands who had their lives changed by the Oxford Group during the 1930's. It is a simple plan of action consisting of Three Assumptions, Four Standards and Four Steps.

Before we begin, we need to know what the Oxford Group was. Many people have never heard of this organization because in the late 1930's it changed its name and shifted its focus.

In the mid 1930's, the Oxford Group was an effective and popular spiritual movement. Then, the Group became ideologically rather than spiritually based. I describe this shift in focus as moving from "Changing the world one life at a time" to "Changing the world one country at a time." The purpose of this book is to take you back to the original Oxford Group program–the program that existed during the height of its success.

Let us start by taking a look at how the Group perceived itself. The principles and precepts of the movement were clearly defined in the opening lines of the book, *What Is the Oxford Group?* This book was written anonymously in 1933:

You cannot belong to the Group. It has no membership list, subscriptions, badge, rules or definite location. It is a name for a group of people who, from every rank, profession, and trade, in many countries, have surrendered their lives to God and who are endeavoring to lead a spiritual quality of life under the guidance of the Holy Spirit.

The Group is not a religion; it has no hierarchy, no temples, no endowments; its workers have no salaries, no plans but God's plan; every country is their country, every man and woman their brother and sister.

The Group advocates nothing that is not the fundamental basis of all Faith, and takes no side in sectarian disputes. It enables us to use our beliefs to their best advantage for ourselves and for the world in general. This means living, as near as we can, to the life God has mapped out for us. Divine Guidance shows us how we can best do this, so we can follow God's plan and bring it to fruition.
(*What Is the Oxford Group?*, pp. 3-4, edited)

The Group was not a religion. It did not get involved in interpreting the Bible or practicing church rituals. The organization was not concerned with saving souls, rather, it was concerned with changing lives.

The Group increased the world's awareness of a living God and the value of two-way prayer. The program released people from addictive and compulsive behaviors. All Twelve Step programs evolved from this highly successful approach, which was based on the establishment and maintenance of an intimate, two-way communication with "the One who has all power."

We will begin our spiritual journey by examining the assumptions upon which the program was built. Next, we will present the Four Standards. Then we will take the Four Steps of Surrender, Sharing, Restitution and Guidance.

By following this process, we will remove the barriers that have separated us from our Creator. We will establish a bridge to God and those around us. This will produce the psychic change that results from knowing we are "a part of" rather than "apart from." The Steps will provide the spiritual solution to all of our problems.

First, we need to look at the assumptions. They are:

1. God speaks!

2. God has a plan for our lives.

3. God will reveal this plan to us, if we are willing to listen and follow directions.

Before we proceed, we need a clear understanding of some of the basic spiritual principles upon which these assumptions are based. Let us start with the concept of God.

We must be careful not to let prejudice or "contempt prior to investigation" prevent us from receiving the full benefit of two-way prayer. The God we are referring to is the Voice within.

We are free to call this Voice by any name we feel comfortable with as long as it does not represent something or someone outside of us. We are not talking about the "god" of the lightbulb, the doorknob, the tarot card or the astrology chart. All of these are external manifestations of self. We are talking about the Creator-the Spirit of the Universe that resides within each and every one of us. This Inner Voice has been given many names throughout the ages. For convenience, we will call this voice God.

Not everything we hear comes from God. There is another voice that resides within us-the voice that separates us from God and keeps us in total darkness. This voice has also been described and discussed at length. We will call this voice Self.

Some say there is only one voice and it is the voice of our conscience. James Houck effectively counters this point of view when he tells us, "Conscience can tell the difference between right and wrong, but, only Divine Guidance can tell the difference between two rights."

The concept of listening to God is as old as recorded history. Throughout the ages, men and women have been listening to the Voice within. Some have taken the time to record what they have heard. These writings have been incorporated into many of the religious books of the world.

This is a very small sample of what has been written:

God speaks!

> Speak, LORD, for your servant hears.
> *1 Samuel 3:9*

> I will hear what God the LORD will speak, . . .
> *Psalm 85:8*

He calls his own sheep by name, and leads them out.

And the sheep follow him: for they know his voice.

John 10:3-4

Meditate on thy Lord in thine own heart, with humility and without loud speaking, evening and morning.

The Koran

God has a plan for our lives.

Teach me Your way, O LORD; I will walk in Your truth.

Psalm 86:11

When He, the Spirit of truth, has come, He will guide you into all truth.

John 16:13

In the rush and noise of life, as you have intervals, step within yourselves and be still. Wait upon God and feel His good presence: this will carry you evenly through your day's business.

William Penn (Quaker)

God will reveal this plan to us if we are willing to listen and follow directions.

I will instruct you and teach you in the way you should go.

Psalm 32:8

This word came unto Jeremiah from the LORD,

saying: Take a scroll of a book, and write on it all the words that I have spoken to you.

Jeremiah 36:1-2

For there is nothing covered that will not be revealed, nor hidden that will not be known.

Luke 12:2

An hour of listening is better than a thousand years of prayer.

The Koran

Anyone who withdraws into meditation on compassion can see Brahma with his own eyes, talk to him face to face and consult with him.

Digha Nikaya 19.43

The strongest memory is weaker than the palest ink.

Chinese Proverb

In the 1920 and 1930's, many Oxford Group authors wrote about listening to the "God who speaks." Some of these books are:

When Man Listens, by Cecil Rose
The God Who Speaks, by Burnett Hillman Streeter
God Does Guide Us, by W. E. Sangster
How Do I Begin?, by Hallen Viney (pamphlet)
How to Listen to God, by John Batterson (pamphlet)
The Guidance of God, by Eleanor Forde-Newton

We will use excerpts from these sources to explain our assumptions in greater detail. We hope you will find the passages to be spirit filled and just as relevant today as when they were written.

God speaks!

Cecil Rose, an English member of the Group, wrote *When Man Listens* in 1937. In this book, he maintains that God has spoken throughout the ages:

> How can we receive direction from God? The answer to this question lies in one of the great affirmations of faith: *God speaks*. That is the tremendous fact around which both the Old and New Testaments are built—not that man can and may speak to God, but that God can and does speak to man.
> (*When Man Listens*, p. 27, edited)

In 1930, Eleanor Forde-Newton wrote a 28-page booklet titled *The Guidance of God* within which she describes the "God who speaks":

> Within the Bible, running through the dark perplexing panorama of time, is a stream of communication with the unseen world of the Spirit. Men talked with God. What is more important, God talked with men. Conversations took place and were recorded because they knew God to be a personal Spirit. These were the ones who knew Him intimately.
> (*The Guidance of God*, p. 3, edited)

When bringing up the subject of the "God who speaks," we are sometimes asked, "What language does God use?" Since God speaks to us through our thoughts, God uses our own language–words that we can understand. God talks in a way that will get our attention, if we are listening:

> The Holy spirit is not limited to conventional
> phraseology. God uses the language of the person to
> whom He speaks.
> (*The Guidance of God,* p. 15, edited)

We realize there are many who are skeptical about the
concept of the "God who speaks." However, when asked, these
people invariably tell us they have never tried to listen. They
have never taken the time to clear the channel so they can
experience the benefit of this miraculous spiritual transformation:

> For those who have no experience listening to
> God, denial will come easy. But it is perilous to deny
> anything based on the lack of personal experience.
> These people deny the reality of two-way prayer
> simply because they've never had the faith to try it,
> never experienced it, never submitted to the discipline
> of it. But it is real–as real as God, and as free as God's
> love.
> (*God Does Guide Us,* p. 23, edited)

Even those of us who practice two-way prayer on a regular
basis find that, from time to time, we hear only the incessant
chatter of self-thoughts. Sometimes our fears, frustrations and
anxieties take over and block us from the word of God:

> Not every day is the voice equally clear. The
> closeness of our walk with God determines that. Yet,
> again and again, the special word will speak clearly in
> the soul, and assure the adoring disciple of his way.
> Thousands more are learning to know it at this very
> time. The art of listening is being rediscovered by our

own generation–a practice that needs to be encouraged.
(*God Does Guide Us*, p. 40, edited)

Then, there are those who pray but never take the time to listen. This is not two-way prayer, but rather, a monolog with us doing all the talking. We may enjoy the sound of our own voice, but we accomplish very little in terms of changing ourselves and those around us:

> "I have never heard the Voice," says a disciple, "and I have prayed." But have you persisted in prayer and have you prayed *believing* that God will speak to you? It is possible to pray, and pray often, with no expectation of a reply. The listening side of prayer has been totally neglected. Many people fill every moment of their devotions by talking. No real fellowship is possible under such circumstances, because it is so pitifully one-sided. Common courtesy requires that we listen as well as speak. A sense of reverence and need ought to keep us silent and attentive in the presence of God.
> (*God Does Guide Us*, p. 40)

Victor Kitchen, in *I Was a Pagan*, describes a person who, like so many of us, is a noise junkie–an activity addict. This person has so many conversations going on in his head, he cannot even begin to hear the Voice of God:

> This man is so vividly conscious of his own likes, aversions and dislikes that he literally cannot become conscious of any other thoughts. They make so much "noise" within him that he cannot hear any other "voice."
> (*I Was a Pagan*, p. 44, edited)

If we want to hear the Voice of God, we must take the time to listen. We cannot be preoccupied or let our mind become cluttered with thoughts about self:

God speaks. But if God is to be heard and His plan is to be known and carried out, *man must listen.*

That means a new approach to God for many of us. In the past, our attitude has been, "Listen, Lord for Thy servant speaks." Our prayer has been what B. H. Streeter calls "pagan" prayer — the attempt to bend God to our desires and make God the servant of our needs. We have made our plans and decisions first, and then sought God's blessing and assistance. This one-sided address by us to God is unproductive, so eventually we drop it and complain that prayer doesn't work

In order for prayer to be successful, we must begin with the desire to know God's will for us and be brought under His control. Our petitions will be answered only if we have first placed ourselves in line with His will. If God is to direct our lives, it is vital that we should learn how to listen.
(*When Man Listens,* p. 30, edited)

Martin Luther describes the value of listening to God this way: "One word of His is better than a thousand words of ours." This is why we must learn to listen.

We may hear unexpected or unsolicited things, but when God directs us to do something, we must take action or else the channel will be closed to us in the future. This is where we apply the Four Steps to convert our deficiencies into assets, to right our wrongs, so we can continue to hear the Voice within:

> There is one condition to be fulfilled before we
> begin. We must be willing to hear anything God says
> to us. It is useless to seek His guidance in one area of
> life when we are not prepared for Him to talk to us
> about certain other areas in which we need to deal
> first. If we want guidance about our family, we may
> have to listen to some thing God has to tell us about
> ourselves–our character and habits. If it is personal
> problems, worries or health for which we seek direc-
> tion, we may have to face what God has to say about
> the way we run our business, or about our attitude
> toward money. It is all or nothing. Before we begin to
> listen to God, we must be rid of any known
> reservations.
> (*When Man Listens*, p. 31, edited)

Cecil Rose tells us there are certain Steps we must take in order to become an effective listener. A very important one of these is Restitution:

> Our aim, remember, is to put our life under God's
> control, and find out whether He can speak clearly
> enough in our heart for us to know the steps He
> wants us to take. In all probability there are things
> which will have to be cleared up before God can really
> take control. And the first word God says to us will
> be about these. At any rate let us begin by sitting
> quietly for a few minutes thinking of our life in the
> light of what we already know of God's will.
> (*When Man Listens*, p. 32)

Many of us have become separated from the source of all knowledge and power because we have been listening to the voice of self rather than the Voice of God. Only God can guide and provide for our every need. Only God can remove the manifestations of self that have prevented us from realizing the health, happiness and harmony we have been searching for all our lives.

Even though God speaks, we must surrender in order to hear what God has to say. We must surrender our lives, totally and completely, if we are to become effective listeners:

> The promise that our petitions will be answered is only for those who have first placed themselves in line with God's will. If God is to become for us the living, active God, directing our life, it is vital that we should learn how to listen.
> (*When Man Listens*, p. 31, edited)

God has a plan for our lives.

Now that we have established there is a living God who speaks, we need to look at why God would want to speak to us. It is because God has a plan for our lives–a plan far better than anything we ever could imagine–a plan that will provide serenity, happiness and success beyond anything we ever could have envisioned on our own:

> God *has a plan*. That is one of the great affirmations of Faith.

> In that plan each of us has a part. All the world's troubles and all our own troubles arise from our failure to discover that plan and our part in it. God's plan is the only one on which either society or our own lives will work.
> (*When Man Listens*, p. 25, edited)

The Oxford University theologian and Group supporter, B. H. Streeter expands upon this premise:

> It is a contradiction in terms to say that God exists but has no plan. And to say that His plan can only contemplate the big outline and not also minor detail, is to reduce His intelligence to the scale of ours. It follows from the very nature of God, if there be a God at all; that he differs from man precisely in the fact that He can give attention to everything, everywhere, always and all at once.
> (*The God Who Speaks*, p. 15)

Again, we encounter the skeptics of the world. Even after we have convinced them that God speaks, they protest that God will not speak to them:

> On the other hand, there are those who are so apprehensive about God that they shrink from anything so definite as is implied by the word "plan." They may affirm that the Universe has purpose, or that "values are real"and even admit that God exists; but they feel that God ought to be described in vague and abstract terms. This is another fallacy of the imagination. We ought to talk about God in the fullest and most concrete of terms. That is why we ought to speak of God as "personal."
> (*The God Who Speaks*, pp. 15-16)

If God has purpose, then, most assuredly, we have purpose. From this, we can infer that God has a personal plan just for us. Victor Kitchen describes this plan as follows:

> I figured there must be some purpose for living.

If I live in the hope of being a little more help–or in the hope of serving some higher plan which I do not understand–I would, whether I admitted it or not, be living for a purpose.

If I followed the wrong plan by listening to the wrong voice, as I had most of my life, I would, of course, prove to be of mighty little use to the world and, probably, fail entirely to render any higher service.
(*I Was a Pagan*, p. 12, edited)

As is the case with other aspects of duality, we are free to follow either of two plans–God's plan or our plan. The choice is ours.

In *I Was a Pagan*, a Group member explains this duality to Victor Kitchen:

"You say you believe there is a plan," the Group member continued. "But did it never occur to you to get in touch with the Author of that plan, asking God directly what His plan *is* and what He wants you to *do* about it?"
(*I Was a Pagan*, pp. 55-56, edited)

Victor Kitchen describes his original design for living as the "Five P's." In actuality, this plan had become his design for dying:

I and most of the world had been following the unfortunate "Five P's," of Pleasure, Possessions, Power, Position and Praise. It is a plan–"a design for living" which can best be described as "Egoism." This egoism had left me and most other people that I know

with a great big unfilled gap in our lives. Century after century and generation after generation egoism had brought the world to recurring states of chaos. This being the case, was it not likely that some other untried or less tried plan would prove to be the right one?
(*I Was a Pagan*, p. 13, edited)

The untried or less tried plan Victor writes about is two-way prayer. We have two designs for living–our plan and God's plan. God has given us the free will to follow either one of these plans. The problem is that so many of us chose the plan of self-will which leaves us emotionally defeated and spiritually bankrupt:

There are no misfits in God's plan. The tragedy is when God's plan is missed. There are broken homes, growing estrangements and lifelong mis-understandings; divorces; illegitimate children; nervous breakdowns; ideals scrapped and faith forsaken. This is only some of the wreckage in the lives of people who have not let God chart and compass their lives. The miracle is that God cares, and that, even in the face of such ruin, God can "make all things new."
(*The Guidance of God*, p. 19, edited)

God will reveal this plan to us, if we are willing to listen and follow directions.

Now that we have reached the point where we accept that "God speaks" and that "God has a plan for us," it is time to put God's plan into action:

Not for one single day

Can I discern my way,
But this I surely know–
Who gives the day,
Will show the way,
So I securely go.

–John Oxenham

B. H. Streeter writes that we need to accept and execute to the best of our ability, the entire plan–not just bits and pieces that agree with our self plan:

Once we realize that God has a plan, it becomes self-evident that the only sensible course to take is to ask what God's plan is for us and then endeavor to carry out that plan. For if we can discern anything of God's plan for us, common sense demands that we give ourselves entirely to it.

Here again, human frailty suggests a compromise; we all would like to live partly in accordance with God's plan and partly in accord with our own. But in carrying out God's plan, there can be no half measures. We cannot "split the difference," as they say.

(*The God Who Speaks*, p.17, edited)

It is important that we realize that we do not need to know God's plan for the entire world, or even God's complete plan for us. God will disclose what we need to know in order to carry out that portion of the plan we need to accomplish today:

But at this point someone will say, how am I to know all of God's plan? There is no need to know God's plan in its entirety. All I need to know is God's plan for *me*. Nor do I need to know the details of that plan for my whole future, or even for a year ahead. It is enough to know it day by day.

But, it will be asked, how am I to know even this much? All of us, surely, have such knowledge in the negative sense. We all know at least one thing in our lives which is *not* right–which is contrary to God's plan for us. Until we have straightened out that wrong, it is futile to ask what the next item in God's plan may be. However, if we are ready to confess and make restitution for the wrong of which we are aware, then experience shows that the "still small voice" of "the Beyond that is within" will tell us the next thing that God wishes us to do.
(*The God Who Speaks*, pp. 20-21, edited)

How do we know we are hearing the Voice of God? Here is where we need to practice, practice, practice:

Men and women who have long made a practice of listening to God claim that they can distinguish between their own imagination and God's will. They do not claim that this gift fell upon them suddenly. It is the product of long practice in the art of listening, and they recommend such constant practice to all who would like to possess this precious gift.

God has sometimes spoken clearly to men who had no background in the devotional life, but the rule still holds that those who wish to cultivate the power to know God's voice must set time aside specifically for it, and set it aside every day.
(*God Does Guide Us*, pp. 34-35, edited)

Victor Kitchen was skeptical that God's plan could be revealed to him. He had tried to pray, but to no avail. Then he realized he had to change his approach:

> I had previously failed to learn God's plan for the very simple reason that I had been trying to supply all the power myself–even after I learned that power for spiritual growth would have to come from the inside.
>
> The idea of getting directly in touch with God–by asking questions and getting answers and directions for the conduct of my life–seemed to me an out-and-out absurdity.
>
> Yet these people said it could be done. They said they were doing it themselves and that was what gave them the power to *apply* beliefs and *carry out* the plan of God–a power that I did not have. They said, however that I could have it–just as they did–if I would pay the same price–comply with the same conditions–and go through the same series of exceedingly simple steps.
> (*I Was a Pagan*, pp. 39, 56, edited)

Here Victor provides us with the insight necessary to carry out God's plan. We must take a series of Steps. The Steps are Surrender, Sharing, Restitution and Guidance.

Cecil Rose also tells us we need to implement the plan we have received from God or else we will lose our direct line of communication with our Creator:

> If we want to go on with it we had better carry out these first orders which have come to us, for God can only continue to speak to us if we obey. Dis-

obedience blocks the line.
(*When Man Listens*, p. 32)

Eleanor Forde-Newton writes about God's plan with respect to the Four Standards of Honesty, Purity, Unselfishness and Love. We use this test to separate God's plan from our own plan:

> The God directed plan has signposts. The first is the spiritual test found in the Sermon on the Mount. This test is steeped in the experience of men and women who, throughout the centuries, have dared to live under divine revelation. These people identify themselves with God's redemptive work by living a life that is completely honest, pure, unselfish, loving.

> The second signpost is faith. The guided life calls for great human risks and much trail blazing. Life under God's hand often calls us to act upon probabilities rather than upon certainties.

> The third guidepost is fellowship. What say others to whom God speaks? This calls for the death of spiritual pride. In God's plan there is no place for the temperamental whims of the person who likes to play the rogue elephant and resents the constraining discipline of the "team." This person's loyalty has no wider scope than his vanity. We must be prepared to let any plan of our own, however good, be superseded, if God reveals a better one through other people.
> (*The Guidance of God*, pp. 19, 20, 21-22, edited)

In a world where people who worship the power of self are trying to eliminate all moral and ethical principles from our society, it is a revelation to know there are some universal guidelines which will keep us from being drawn into the abyss of addiction, compulsion and selfishness. These guidelines are the Four Standards.

6

The Four Standards

We have established that God speaks, God has a plan for our lives, and God will reveal this plan to us if we are willing to listen and follow directions. Next, we examine the thoughts that enter our mind when we listen to the "God who speaks." How do we know we are listening to the voice of God? How do we distinguish the God thoughts from the self-thoughts?

We are most fortunate, because the Group provides us with a very simple, straightforward way to check what we hear so we can determine the source. The test consists of the Four Standards of Honesty, Purity, Unselfishness and Love.

We can use this test to judge everything we think, say or do. Some people have described these Standards as absolutes or ideals. Whether we call them Standards or absolutes, they are fundamentally sound spiritual principles that are consistent with the teachings of the major religions of the world:

The Group has four points which are the keys to the kind of spiritual life God wishes us to lead. These points are:

1. Honesty

2. Purity
3. Unselfishness
4. Love
(*What Is the Oxford Group?*, p. 7, edited)

This test was developed by Robert E. Spear. In 1902, he wrote a book titled *The Principles of Jesus* in which he examined the teachings found in the Sermon on the Mount (Matthew 5:1 - 7:29). He summarized this "design for living" into four categories which he called "points of application." They were truth, unselfishness, purity and love. Later these principles were modified into the Four Standards as we know them today: Honesty, Purity, Unselfishness and Love.

Victor Kitchen, the author of *I was a Pagan*, describes the Four Standards as well as their opposites. By looking at both the positive and negative sides of the test, we get a clearer picture of how to separate God's will from self-will:

> He is not made up, like an intellectual giant, of doctor's degrees and learned societies. He is made up of the simple moral qualities of Honesty, Purity, Unselfishness and Love.

> He does not grow more honest or more pure by increasing his knowledge of what is honest and pure. He does not "get that way" through his intellect at all. Nor does he become more honest and pure through his physical prowess and achievements.

> All the material possessions I have ever acquired and all the intellectual knowledge I have ever gathered, have not added a single cubit to my moral stature. In fact, if anything, I have grown through the years more dishonest, more impure, more selfish and

more unloving than ever.
(*I Was a Pagan*, pp. 21, 23, edited)

Let us take a closer look at this simple test we can use to separate the God thoughts from the self-thoughts when we are practicing two-way prayer. If what we hear is Honest, Pure, Unselfish and Loving, there is a good chance these thoughts are from God. Conversely, if what we hear is dishonest, impure, selfish and unloving, we can be equally assured these thoughts are from self.

This test can be illustrated as a series of questions to separate God's will from self-will.

Honesty	**Is it true or false?**
Purity	**Is it right or wrong?**
Unselfishness	**Is it God directed or self-directed?**
Love	**Is it based in faith or fear?**

As E. Stanley Jones writes in *Victorious Living*, we need to take actions in order to convert the barriers which separate us from God and those around us to the bridges of two-way prayer and two-way sharing:

> The barriers to finding God are not on God's side, but on ours. Since God is seeking us, then the problem is not of our finding God, but of our letting God find us. We must put ourselves in the way of being found by God. Some of us try to hide from God to avoid being found. The barriers are definitely on our side.
> (*Victorious Living*, p. 35, edited)

Cecil Rose, the author of *When Man Listens*, summarizes the Four Standards as follows:

Is it True or False?

Honesty? Well, that is not so bad. I do not rob the till, or make fraudulent returns to the Internal Revenue Service. But absolute Honesty? That looks different. Do I make elaborate excuses over something that I have simply forgotten to do? Do I waste my employer's time by lateness or negligence? Am I completely open with the members of my family?
(*When Man Listens*, p. 18, edited)

Is it Right or Wrong?

Purity? What would my thought-life look like projected onto a movie screen?
(*When Man Listens*, p. 18, edited)

Is it God Directed or Self-Directed?

Unselfishness? Am I thinking of others, or am I only thinking about my own feelings and reputation? Do I get touchy and defensive when people criticize me? And what would my family say about my unselfishness?
(*When Man Listens*, p. 18, edited)

Is it based in Faith or Fear?

Love? Yes, I know that I did not begin the trouble, and as far as I know, have done nothing to keep it going, but what have I done to end it? And what about my likes and dislikes?
(*When Man Listens*, pp. 18-19)

Now let us look at each of the Four Standards in more

detail.

Honesty

The search for truth is at the heart of our spiritual journey. To discover a great new principle or discard an old prejudice can result in an entirely new outlook on life. When we are not actively seeking truth, we are in danger of letting falsehood control our thoughts. Veracity is as much the source of everlasting life as fallacy is the source of spiritual death. It is the eternal, unrelenting desire for truth that counts. It has to be the focus of our attention.

Over and over we must ask ourselves, "Is it true or is it false? The real virtue in honesty lies in the persistent dedicated striving for it. Our unrelenting pursuit of truth sets us free, even if we do not quite reach our goal. On the other hand, we do not have to pursue the false. All we have to do is relax our pursuit of the truth, and that which is false will find us.

E. Stanley Jones describes honesty in the following manner:

Can we be absolutely trusted in money matters? In our work? With other people's reputations?

It is not easy to be absolutely honest with ourselves because of our tendency to rationalize. This means that we are seldom objective in our attitudes toward ourselves. We set our minds to work, not upon the facts as they are, but upon the business of inventing reasons for our courses of conduct. The mind plays tricks on us. We are self-deceived.

We must be willing to cut out–ruthlessly cut out of our lives–every dishonest thing no matter how

deep the embarrassment or humiliation may be.
(*Victorious Living*, pp. 36, 38, edited)

It is much simpler to appear honest, than to be honest. We must strive to be what we appear to be. It is easier to be honest with others than with ourselves. Our searching and fearless moral inventories are invaluable, because, if we truly are seekers of truth, we will become more honest by just going through the process.

We must get honest about our tongue, our actions and our attitude. As for our tongue, E. Stanley Jones provides us with this insight:

> Are there any conditions under which we will or do tell a lie? Can we be depended on to tell the truth, no matter the cost?
>
> Whether or not we will lie is a test of our character. And yet how easy it is to lie–even for the most spiritual of us: the willingness to twist a meaning to gain a point, to misquote if the misquotation gains an end, exaggerations to make impressions, a lack of complete truth in making appeals for funds, misrepresentations in presenting goods for sale. What is at the basis of this looseness with the truth? Is it not often in the fact that we think a lie is sometimes justifiable?
>
> Hold onto these two principles. First, God cannot lie. Second, God cannot delegate to us the privilege of lying for Him. Truth is sacred. Lies separate us from God's will. If we still lie, no matter how spiritual we may be, we remain in our old, self-defeating life
> (*Victorious Living*, pp. 36-37, edited)

But we must not use honesty as a weapon to hurt others. We temper our pursuit of the truth with a genuine concern for the welfare of others:

> Under God's guidance, truthfulness is tempered with common sense and kindliness. "Love thy neighbor as thyself" is a sufficient test of our motives for honesty. There is no reason why, in our desire to be honest with God, we should hurt other people. God-given discretion is better than our unloving determination to be honest at all costs, mostly other people's.
> (*What Is the Oxford Group?*, p. 76, edited)

Love is the spring from which all true honesty flows. If we truly love other people, we will be sincere, as well as honest in our dealings with them:

> Many people revel in what they think is absolute Honesty. They are convinced that it means telling the bald, unvarnished facts about themselves even if it involves other people. If the truth is without consideration or discretion, it is better to keep a silent tongue and await the decision of our guidance than to blurt out what may be a truth but a truth which will send a person even farther away from us. Truth should not be destructive, but spiritually constructive. Honesty is not, of necessity, criticism.
> (*What Is the Oxford Group?*, p. 77, edited)

The family must practice honesty if it is to remain united. Deception and avoidance of truthful discussions about hopes, dreams, needs and wants can only lead to emotional separation and, eventually, physical divorce:

How can any husband or wife live in perfect understanding if either has a secret which, should it come to light from an outside source, will wreck their partnership? Reluctance to be honest about our faults, mistakes or transgressions with the person we are united to by love is lack of faith, not only in that person but also in the reality of that love. A love which dies because one confesses, with honest motives, a misdeed to the other is not worth having, and any love which can embrace mutual honesty is very near to the ideal which God had for men and women when God ordained marriage.
(*What Is the Oxford Group?*, p. 78, edited)

We also must be honest with our friends. This is a test of true friendship. Can we be truthful with these people or are we afraid to let them know what we really think or feel? If we cannot tell these people the truth about ourselves, they are not our friends. They are either acquaintances or people we are using to feed our ego or to further our selfish objectives:

Honesty with our friends is necessary if we are to know we can rely on them to stand with us in an emergency.
(*What Is the Oxford Group?*, p. 79)

And, we must be honest in our business dealings. For some of us this may be the most difficult area of all in which to be honest:

In business today, which for most people is one big fight for bare existence let alone profit, honesty has become a forgotten entity. Cut throat competition, false trading representations, underhanded methods of salesmanship and the lack of capital worry thousands into premature old age and disillusion. "Do others before they can do you" is the slogan of the modern business world. But does it bring lasting fruits to anyone? The natural wealth of the world is neither ours nor theirs; it is God's. We are all stewards to God, for His property, by His permission.

As that is so, why should we be so ridiculous as to think we can prosper to any real extent if we use dishonest methods to gain undue possession of the wealth which at its source is absolute Honesty? The popular belief is that honesty cannot go hand in hand with business. But it can. Many of the Group who are in business are witnesses to the fact that honesty not only makes for the right kind of business with a fair profit, but gains them friends in the process. Any astute business person knows that a friend in the business world is a considerable asset.
(*What Is the Oxford Group?*, p. 79, edited)

Since everything on earth belongs to God, we need to develop the faith and confidence that our Creator will provide for us. "When God guides, God provides."

Purity

Blessed are the pure in heart, for they shall see God.
(*Matthew 5:8*)

Purity is simply living the way God wants us to live, completely free from that which corrupts, weakens or contaminates. In this sense purity is related to honesty. Purity is being honest to the best of our ability about what is beneficial for us mentally, physically and spiritually.

In purity as in honesty the virtue lies in the striving. And just as we seek the truth, if we give our all in the constant pursuit of righteousness, we will be free even though we may never quite achieve our objective. The pursuit is a thrilling and challenging journey. The journey is just as important as the destination, however slow it may seem.

We need to ask ourselves, "Is it right or is it wrong?" Are our motives pure in all of our affairs? Do we long for or obsess about the dark-side, in act or in thought?

We need to address purity in terms of mind, body and soul. A wholesome mind in a healthy body that tries to be fair and ethical in business, in work and play, in the use of our possessions, and in our attitudes toward relations, friends and acquaintances is essential if we are to maintain a wholesome relationship with God and our peers.

In the realm of the heart and spirit we face difficulty. Each of us has an intuitive sense as to what is right, but do we have the dedicated will to do it? We must have a determined desire to do that which we know is right, if we are to achieve any measurable degree of purity.

E Stanley Jones provides us with a series of questions we need to ask ourselves about our conduct:

Am I pure in my relationships with the opposite sex? In my habits? In my thought life?

Obviously, the first thing to do in this matter of purity is to acknowledge the fact of sex. To act as though there is no such thing as sex-desires in us is to repress them, and a complex is set up in the subconscious. This leads to nervous trouble and psychological breakdown.

Sex-desire is one of our basic instincts. There is no shame in this. The question is not whether we have sex-desire, but whether sex-desire has us. As a servant of the higher purposes of life, sex-desire is a wonderful servant, giving drive and beauty to the rest of life. As a master, it is hell. Have we victory or defeat over our sex-desire? Am I becoming corrupt in act or in thought? If so, will I surrender it, now? (*Victorious Living*, pp. 36, 39, edited)

In *What Is the Oxford Group?*, the anonymous author of the Group textbook for living describes purity in a way that is timeless. Considering these words were written almost seventy years ago, it is truly amazing how relevant they still are today:

Life today revolves round impurity of thought, motives, and conduct. "Keep moving at all costs"! is the cry that goes up without ceasing day and night. "Don't stand still or you'll be knocked down and trampled on"! "Knock the other person down before he can strike a blow at you"! "He intends to rob you so why not rob him first"?

And so the world races round. Publicity which is mistaken for honesty; moral dirt, physical degeneracy, lying, swindling, adultery; they are not impurities the moderns say. In this world where everything is speed and everything is judged by its financial value, they are considered assets. Souls are for sale cheap. No wonder some of us ask how we can possibly live or think purely when the modern paganism of the world is all around us. Some say it is silly and a waste of time to try it.

Of course, if we do not know peace, or want to
know it, we do not realize the Power of the Holy Spirit
to remove temptation and give back in return, true
happiness and peace of mind. The pure in heart not
only see God but hear Him. They know that seeking
Purity is never in vain.
(*What Is the Oxford Group?*, pp. 88, 89, edited)

The advertising industry appeals to and exploits our sex-
desires to sell us products and services.   Sexual imagery
permeates every facet of the commercial world. Sex is sold as
a substitute for love–a way to fill the void in an otherwise
meaningless and unfulfilled life based on selfishness.

For many, the constant pursuit of sexual gratification
becomes an addiction. Like any other addiction, an obsession
with sex separates us from God:

To some, sex is everything; their world revolves
around it and all its trappings. Sex is love to them;
their escape from an otherwise humdrum world.
They earn money for it; dress for it; live for it and
dream of it. Without this all consuming sex obsession, they can conceive of no life possible for them.
Everything they do is traceable to sex-domination.

"Impurity? What is that?" they ask. There is no such
word as impurity to those who have made sex their
god.
(*What Is the Oxford Group?*, p. 89, edited)

Many people, who lack clearly defined moral values, are in
positions of influence in both the public and private sectors of
our nation. As a consequence, we are witnessing an alarming
increase in divorce and adolescent drug and alcohol abuse. We

are paying a terrible price for the selfish indulgences of our political and social leaders:

> With certain sets of people who call themselves "intellectuals" impurity has become the fashion. A number of these "intellectuals" are really mental snobs who have a total disregard for the moral values upon which a healthy community is built. Writers of a certain class of fiction decry all forms of decency and purity, deceiving the reading public into believing that if they put expressions and words that are not usually used in decent society into print, it is a sign of genius.
> (*What Is the Oxford Group?*, p. 91, edited)

The media is filled with messages that "Greed is good" and sex is its own reward. These communications are an attempt to lead people further and further away from the spiritual solution to their problems:

> The theater and cinema are easy prey to those who would commercialize indecencies. That pictorial art must shock to attract attention is the belief of some of those who have an artistic capacity.
> (*What Is the Oxford Group?*, pp. 91-92)

It is the removal of God from the business world that has resulted in inferior products and environmental destruction, all in the name of profit and prosperity:

> How can we have untainted motives in the business world, for instance, when we have to compete with the lying misrepresentations of our competitors who will stop at nothing to ruin us? How can we think modestly when literature, films, plays

and art rely on impurity to tickle the palate of a jaded public? How can we behave with purity when we are surrounded by people who find impurity of action to be the order of the day? They say, "we are not on earth forever" and "live today for tomorrow we may die."

How many people believe that though the world breeds impurity God can take it away? If we believe God can overcome every temptation, we must believe that God can keep us pure. He has never allowed a soul to suffer for resisting a temptation.

Feeding the mind impurities is like feeding the body tainted food. Because we know the consequences to the body of such foolishness, we would not eat spoiled food. Why then do we feed the mind contaminated food that will slowly but surely destroy the soul? Destroy it until, because the Holy Spirit has been overcome within us, we say bitterly there is no God?
(*What Is the Oxford Group?*, p. 92, edited)

It is from the mouths of those who have lost all contact with the Holy Spirit that we hear, "God is dead!" But, as we most certainly know, God is very much alive inside each and every one of us. Those that cannot or will not acknowledge God are the ones who are dead–submerged in the depths of loneliness and despair–without the benefit of the all loving, all forgiving, all powerful God.

Unselfishness

We must give to others in order to sustain our own spiritual growth. Setting our own interests aside and directing our attention to the needs of others, without thought of our own satisfaction or reward, is the essence of unselfishness

We need to ask, "Who are we living for?" Is it for ourselves–our "little plans and designs," or is it for others–to see "what we could pack into the stream of life." In the final analysis, we have to determine what controls our actions–is it self-interest or is it God interest? In the depth of our soul, who gives the final word? Are we self-directed or God directed?

Selfishness is the consequence of allowing our spiritual and material possessions to possess us. A. J. Russell likens selfishness to watching our own movie:

> A young lady once told us she had a private movie projector tucked away in the back of her head. When her mind was not otherwise occupied, she would set the film in motion and delight to watch scene after scene, of romance, tragedy, adventure and heroism, in each of which she herself was the central figure. It finally concluded in the imaginary scene in which her own deepest desires were fully gratified. All of us have our daydreams in one form or another. Though not necessarily wrong in and of themselves, in so far as they are centered in self-interest, they are wrong. (*For Sinners Only*, pg 326, edited)

When we take advantage of others to feed our own selfish desires, we end up drowning in greed and obsession. Initially, we may succeed in getting our way but, eventually, we will detest what we have done. If self is in charge, our ultimate reward is disillusionment and discontentment.

The face we portray to the world may be very refined, very moral, even self-sacrificing, but if ego is in command and makes the final decisions, we can be assured that peace and serenity will escape us. Our lives need a Master, but ego is not the master that it needs. It is essential that we move beyond the constant self-thoughts to the quiet serenity of selflessness. The simple question we need to ask ourselves is, "How will this affect the other fellow?"

In *What Is the Oxford Group?*, the author describes unselfishness as a manifestation of love:

> Absolute unselfishness is only possible if we have absolute love; we can only be unselfish according to the love we extend to the object of our unselfishness. Sacrifice of our interests to the interests of others, without thought of reward is, in itself, love, although we may not consciously recognize it as such when we are performing our act of unselfishness. There is more joy in unselfishness than selfish people realize. (*What Is the Oxford Group?*, p 97, edited)

Unselfishness requires that we rise above the pettiness of false pride, jealousy, envy, greed, laziness and prejudice:

> Why are we envious of other people? It does not take a genius to figure this out. We want things other people have that we feel we could appreciate more than they do. We are dissatisfied; life is unfair to us. (*What Is the Oxford Group?*, p. 97, edited))

Jealousy is an emotional firestorm. Not only do our suspicions separate us from God but the manifestations of our jealousy–anger and resentment–can lead to violent outbursts and physical confrontations. This can result in considerable emotional and physical suffering.

Even though jealousy poisons the mind, some of us go to great lengths to feed our suspicions. Even a small and unimportant jealousy can in time become a giant obsession:

> Jealousy, envy and pride, are the causes of our own little wars which we fight with our relations, friends, and neighbors, either in private or in public. Before these petty wars with others can cease, we must make peace within ourselves. We know it is as useless to compete with someone who refuses to compete with us as it is to play a game with someone who will not play. When we stop, the war stops. If we are not interested in pursuing the fight, those who try to keep the battle going find their joy and zest for the confrontation greatly diminished.
> (*What Is the Oxford Group?*, p. 103, edited)

Selfishness is also the source of prejudice toward other races, nationalities or creeds. Until we see the utter futility and self destructiveness of prejudicial thoughts and actions, we will continue to harbor these feelings of ill will toward those around us:

> Selfishness contributes a great deal toward class hatred. Universal waste in these days of glaring poverty is criminal, but who is going to stop it? A man without wealth can be just as selfish as one with a fortune. We can and do waste our physical energies and spiritual possibilities as flagrantly as wealth is wasted. Our spiritual potential for individual and universal good, is wasted in abortive endeavors to make the world a better place by human means alone.
> (*What Is the Oxford Group?*, p. 104, edited)

In order to avoid being drawn into the false illusion that

there is something to be gained from being selfish, we must concentrate on bringing unselfishness into all of our relationships. Let us start by looking at our families:

> In home life, unselfishness is a sure foundation for harmony. It does away with friction and lubricates everything with love. Family feuds, caused by jealousy, pride and suspicion have wrecked many lives. The silly spectacle of two people, closely related, ignoring each other in public because they are playing the hating game is too familiar to some of us to be funny any longer. "It is more blessed to give than to receive." It is miraculous what giving with no thought of return can do to disarm the person who is opposed to us.
> (*What Is the Oxford Group?*, p. 99, edited)

When we lose our selfishness we also lose our self-pity. The "poor-me's" become a thing of the past when we put the thoughts of others ahead of our own:

> The curious thing is that the practice of unselfishness takes away, as if by magic, all the self-pity; all the excuses we make to ourselves for our failures and the feelings that we are being cheated. In return, unselfishness gives us the wonder of an inexplicable spiritual treasure, a description of which is impossible to put into words.
> (*What Is the Oxford Group?*, p. 98)

When we discover this new way of living without thought of self, we become more serene and content. We might even find ourselves happier than we have ever been before. When we reach this state of enlightenment, we sometimes forget there are many others who also could benefit from our new way of living, if we would just take the time to show them how. We guide them to God by listening to their difficulties and demonstrating by simple faith that God is doing for us what we cannot do for ourselves.

Love

Love is the universal language of the heart. It is the emotion that directly connects us to the Holy Spirit within and the world without. Love is a giving and a receiving that transcends all other emotions. The love of God provides us with the strength and direction to change lives and, in so doing, change the world.

Love provides us with the ability to see the unseen, know the unknown and comprehend the incomprehensible. Love allows us to shoulder the burdens of those around us without becoming weary or despondent, and to step out in faith without hesitation or fear:

> This is my commandment, that you love one another
> as I have loved you.
>
> *John 15: 12*

We need to test out thoughts and actions. "Is what I am thinking or doing based in faith or is it based in fear."

Love must be unconditional. God does not discriminate. Why would we do any less if we are trying to follow God's will? It is essential for us to develop a universal love of everyone and everything if we are to become God conscious, because God "makes His sun to rise on the evil and on the good and sends rain on the just and the unjust."

Love cannot be forced. It requires a change in perception.

Our attitude toward life is altered when we stop seeing people as either good or bad, and start seeing them as they really are: children of God with varying degrees of God consciousness.

Love must be voluntary, asking nothing in return. We need to see through the self-centeredness and realize all we have belongs to God. We are only stewards of the material gifts God affords us. We are obligated to use these gifts to help others and to make this world a better place for all.

Love is the ultimate freedom. The moment we try to coerce, control or contradict, love dies. When we try to live up to others expectations, love dies. When we lose our need to control others, we will be free to love them just as they are.

Love is the desire to extend ourselves in order to nurture the spiritual growth of those around us. In so doing, we find ourselves able to live in complete harmony with all that God has created:

> Love is not dependent on any condition; it needs neither vast intellect nor robust physical health to realize and use its unlimited powers. It is not an exclusive gift for the use of one type of individual more than another. It is the one indispensable part of existence that all the wealth there is, or ever has been, cannot buy.
> (*What Is the Oxford Group?*, p. 109, edited)

Love is the absence of fear. Love and fear are the two core emotions from which all other emotions emanate. If we are trapped in fear, there can be no love in either thought or deed:

> The realization that God loves us takes away all fear, doubt, regret and remorse–shame of the past and

dread of the future. Such love transcends all understanding, supplying us with infinite patience,
enduring courage and complete trust in God. If we
could love God with a fraction of the love God has for
us, our eyes would be open to a new vision, not only
for ourselves, but for all of mankind.
(*What Is the Oxford Group?*, p. 110)

Love provides us with the opportunity to better the world
by extending our hand to those in need. By allowing God's love
to radiate through us, we light the way for those who are still
living in the darkness of addiction, depression and despair:

Love is not self-negation; it is using the best of
ourselves for the best of other people and, in so doing,
we realize that the best within us is a positive force for
our own good as well as that of others.
(*What Is the Oxford Group?*, p. 110, edited)

Since love and fear are mutually exclusive emotions, we
need to understand the dark side of love, so we will have a clear
understanding as to what actions are unloving and therefore
not from God:

Bad-tempered, touchy and quarrelsome people
do as much harm to the Kingdom of God as
drunkards or adulterers. We can drive others back
into the darkness by a wrong spirit. If the psychol-
ogist were asked to name the two major sins, from
their point of view, they would probably name fear
and anger. They form the basis for most of our
unhappiness. They are impossible to integrate into a
healthy personality.
(*Victorious Living*, p. 40, edited)

If we let fear run our lives, we are in danger of becoming physically ill as well as emotionally obsessed. Since God has given us free will, we can overcome our fears by choosing to let the loving hand of God keep us safe and protected. When we express love instead of fear, we radiate health and well being.

Love is not only doing for others but understanding our place in God's universe. When we become conscious of other people's existence, we begin to realize our interdependence. We are all separate individuals with our wants, needs, strengths, weaknesses, likes and dislikes. But, if we link our individuality to others in a way that neither we nor they are the weaker or the stronger, we can become partners in mutual understanding and forgiveness and live in perfect harmony. To do this is to understand the principle of unconditional love:

> God can and does give back to us so much more in return than what we give up for our fellows. No person has given up more for humanity than God could repay. Within us all we have the inexhaustible wealth of God to draw on, a wealth which is a treasure within us, a treasure which becomes more precious as we move from the material to the spiritual.
> (*What Is the Oxford Group?*, p. 116, edited)

Honesty, Purity, Unselfishness and Love, these are the principles that enhance our spiritual lives. If we are willing to judge everything we think, say or do in terms of these Four Standards, we will find ourselves "walking hand in hand with the Spirit of the Universe" and growing in our understanding of God's plan for us in the days, weeks, months, and years ahead. It is a beautiful journey–all that is required is the Love necessary to step out in Faith and embrace the Highest Power–the Divine Presence within.

7

Step 1: Surrender

As spiritual beings, it is essential we maintain an intimate two-way relationship with our Creator. God can be our loving Friend and Provider, the Director of all our affairs. When we surrender our will, share our faults, make restitution and follow guidance, we walk "hand in hand with the Spirit of the Universe."

In order to receive the full benefit from this connection to the source of all Power, we faithfully practice living in God's presence. We listen to, test, check and obey the Voice within. By doing so, we learn God's plan for our lives.

We are about to embark on a spiritual journey which will provide us with a new level of awareness. We will move from the problem, which is *us*, to the solution, which is *God*. No matter what our difficulties, our obsessions, our fears, our resentments, our self-destructive behaviors, the solution is the same.

We offer this answer to anyone who is interested in a spiritual way of life. All that is required is to take a few simple Steps that will produce a life-changing alteration in perception. You will be transformed, and you will live a God directed life of purpose and meaning beyond your wildest dreams:

> To be spiritually reborn, and to live in the state in which the Four Standards are the guides to our life with God, we advocate four practical spiritual activities:
>
> 1. *Surrender* our life, past, present and future, into God's care and direction.
>
> 2. *Sharing* with God and another person the characteristics of self, which have separated us from our Creator.
>
> 3. Make *Restitution* to all whom we have wronged, directly or indirectly.
>
> 4. Listen to, accept and rely on God's *Guidance* and carry it out in everything we think, say or do, great or small.
>
> (*What Is the Oxford Group?*, pp. 8-9, edited)

A. J. Russell, a British writer and journalist, describes the Four Step program in his book *For Sinners Only*:

> I was starting to get the hang of the Group principles. First, there was complete **Surrender** of everything–time, possessions, relationships, ambitions–to God. Second, there was **Sharing**, confession to God and to another person to produce a right relationship with the Holy Spirit. Third, there was **Restitution** which often changed the lives of those confessed to as well as the life of the confessor. Fourth, there was **Guidance**, a "listening in" to God for definite messages applicable to present needs. In

addition there were the Four Standards of Honesty, Purity, Unselfishness and Love.
(*For Sinners Only*, pp. 25-26, 42-43, 63, 93, edited)

One of the requirements for a successful transformation from a life run on self-will to a life guided by God's will is to enlist the aid of a sharing partner. We cannot take these Steps alone. This will become quite evident as we start on our journey to God through two-way prayer.

A sharing partner is a person who has taken the Steps, has had the conversion experience, is conducting a daily "quiet time" and is actively working with others. This person will witness our surrender, listen to our inventory, guide us through our restitutions and share guidance with us on a regular basis.

Okay, let us begin.

What Is the Oxford Group? contains an entire chapter on each of the Four Steps. In the chapter titled "Surrender," the author describes this initial Step to a spiritual awakening:

> The act of Surrender is not, in any way, an outward and visible ceremony we feel we must shrink from; it is a simple decision put into simple language spoken aloud to God, in front of a witness, at any time and in any place where we have decided to give our past to God and to place our future in His keeping. Nothing more is needed.
> (*What Is the Oxford Group?*, p. 47, edited)

Surrender is a three part process. First, we must acknowledge we have a problem which has separated us from God. This is a difficult task because we can not see ourselves as others do. This lack of self-perception is exemplified by a Zen poem:

> Like the sword that cuts, but cannot cut itself,
> Like the eye that sees, but cannot see itself.

This is why a "sharing partner" is so important. We are not good judges of character, especially our own. We need to be in regular contact with someone who will help us to see ourselves more clearly.

Second, we must believe there is a God, a Voice within. Some say all we have to do is acknowledge the existence of a "Higher Power." There are many Higher Powers, but most of them produce less than satisfactory results. A few of these Higher Powers are alcohol, drugs, fame, food and fortune. Many of us have worshiped at the altar of these and other "false gods." If we want to overcome our difficulties, we must rely upon the **"Highest Power"** which is **God**. A Higher Power will not suffice under these circumstances.

Third, we must be willing to let God direct our activities. We have done a good job of running our lives aground and now it is time to let someone else steer the boat. It is time to put the One who "sees all and knows all" in charge of keeping us away from the reefs and sandbars of life.

But, many of us do not want to give up control. We see ourselves as the center of the universe. Everything revolves around us. Our perception of the world can be summed up by the last lines of *Invictus* written by William Ernest Henley in the late 19th century:

> It matters not how short the gate,
>   How charged with punishments the scroll.
> I am the master of my fate,

I am the Captain of my soul.

By thinking we are the center of the universe, we separate ourselves from God and our fellows. To become a spiritual force working for a better world, we need to change our perception of reality and put God at the center of everything we do:

> Change of mind—a new way of looking at things — reveals to us that we belong to God and must therefore absolutely surrender ourselves and be entirely at His disposal. The surrender of self must include every interest, possession and relationship.
> (*The Eight Points of the Oxford Group*, p. 8)

Prior to our surrender, many of us lived in a prison of total darkness, seeing the world as a hostile, lonely, frightening place. Once we abandon ourselves to God, we view the world differently because we have been reborn into a new way of living:

> Men and women must realize that living by self-will can kill not only the soul but the mind, talents and happiness as surely as a malignant physical disease can kill the body. Surrender to God, in actuality as well as in theory, means a new lease on life which brings with it a fuller joy of living than they have realized was possible for them. They have been reborn to the world as well as reborn to God.
> (*What Is the Oxford Group?*, p. 4, edited)

We must surrender before we can take the rest of the Steps. It is a decision we make for ourselves–we must be committed to letting God direct us:

> We surrender our lives to God with Absolute
> Honesty and immediately commence to rely with
> Absolute Love on His Guidance for the future
> direction of our surrendered lives. This is such a
> simple fact that it appears intricate to some–as simple
> facts sometimes do. But, in spite of its sounding
> simplicity, Surrender is one of the few things in our
> lives which we cannot have someone else do for us.
> It is an act that can only be performed by the
> individual. To God, who knows each one of us far
> better then we could ever know ourselves, the spirit of
> surrender is of far more importance than the letter.
> (*What Is the Oxford Group?*, p. 42, edited)

Now, let us look at the first part of the surrender process,
which is to acknowledge we are having difficulty trying to live
life on life's terms.

Part 1: We admit we have a problem.

Denial prevents us from realizing that the loneliness and
despair we feel is the direct result of the choice we have made
to live our lives without spiritual assistance. We blame our
difficulties on bad luck, circumstances beyond our control, and
other people. When in denial, we live the lie that we can
control the world and those around us. We never think to look
within for the source of our problems:

> There are growing numbers of men and women
> who cannot adjust themselves to the strains and
> demands of life today. They are the victims of
> anxiety. They fail to solve the problems of sex,
> marriage and home life. They are oppressed by the
> sense of futility in a life for which they see no
> purpose. They cannot understand themselves and are

ill-adjusted to their surroundings and their work. Their real trouble is that they have been trying to run their lives in their own way, by their own wisdom, and by their own strength.
(*When Man Listens*, p. 26, edited)

We must realize that trying to direct our own life "can hardly be a success." We are frustrated and discouraged. We do not realize we are out of sync with God's plan:

First of all, life as we have run it ourselves, has not produced the kind of success for which we can be proud. It is worthwhile giving God the chance to run it better. We have to start our surrender from the place where we happen to be. Sometimes all we can say is, "O God, take charge of my life." If we mean it, God does take control.
(*When Man Listens*, p. 22, edited)

What is God's plan for us? We can only determine this once we realize we do not have all the answers. We must get humble and surrender our life to the One who does have the solution to all our difficulties:

Is there a technique for finding one's life plan? There is. The initial step and the indispensable step in the quest is: **ABSOLUTE SURRENDER OF OUR LIFE TO GOD.** Surrender is "life under new management."
(*The Eight Points of the Oxford Group*, p. 5, edited)

Even those of us who have made a total mess of our lives and have lost many of our physical possessions and cherished relationships can start anew, once we give up the delusion that we are in charge:

It is wonderful what God can do with even a broken life — if He is given all the pieces! Surrender has to be inclusive rather than exclusive.
(*The Eight Points of the Oxford Group*, p. 13)

There is hope even for the most stubborn of us, if we are willing to accept that God control is beneficial–something to be desired and sought:

The surrendered life is not narrow and sickly and impoverished — it is a rich, ample and radiant life. It is not a fumbling, crippled, dingy existence, full of suppressions, prohibitions and exclusions, but rather a life of buoyant vitality and disciplined action.
(*The Eight Points of the Oxford Group*, pg. 13, edited)

We need to realize that surrender is not an admission of defeat. This is difficult for some of us to comprehend, but it is true. We must surrender to win. If we admit we can not do it by ourselves, we will receive the blessings of health, harmony and happiness beyond anything we could have planned by ourselves:

It is not surprising, therefore, that those who have this erroneous conception of God, see submission to Him as a cowardly act when, in fact, it is a courageous decision to do a courageous thing. It takes little or no courage to be a selfish, self-centered sinner, proud of independence and self-will. It requires a tremendous amount of courage to surrender to a world in which we have the very roots of our being, in order to live in the presence of God to the best of our ability.
(*What Is the Oxford Group?*, p. 44, edited)

The first question we need to ask ourselves is:

"Am I willing to admit I have a problem?"

Part 2: We realize God is the solution.

Once we admit we have to take responsibility for our lives and that we cannot fill the "hole in our soul" by ourselves, we must look elsewhere for the answers to our spiritual malady.

Will-power can bring us only so far. We need to rely upon God's power to take us the rest of the way to the spiritual solution to all our difficulties:

> Will-power is an active force, as positive in its effects as say, electricity, even though the effects are beyond our present knowledge. We think that will-power has been the driving force for the accomplishment of great works, deeds, feats and inventions. But in reality, will-power has been insufficient to carry these great projects to completion.
>
> The power for the accomplishment of great achievements comes from God. If our will-power is put under God's direction, it has boundless possibilities. Surrendering our will to God's will does not mean that our faculties are deadened but that they are awakened with the infinite power of God and with the guidance of His judgment for their best use–according to the individual plan He has mapped out for each of us.
> (*What Is the Oxford Group?*, p. 41, edited)

Some will "break and run" at the thought of admitting there is a God. They strengthen their resolve and redouble their efforts to do everything themselves. But eventually, fear, shame and guilt will bring them back to a spiritual way of life, assuming they live through the experience of trying to run their lives without help:

> It is a remarkable fact that many of the skeptics, in spite of their suspicion, often return to the Group–drawn by a power stronger than themselves, which is the power of God. And when they are Changed, as some of them eventually are, they become as supportive of the concept of God as they were formerly critical.
> (*What Is the Oxford Group?*, p. 50, edited)

Many of us have been psychologically damaged by our childhood religious experiences. We find it difficult to accept an all-loving and all-forgiving God. We project our suspicions onto others and we are unable to see beyond the wall of doubt we have built up around ourselves:

> These people suspect others of having faults which they definitely have themselves. The discussion of spiritual matters impels them immediately to look for ulterior motives. When they fail to find these, they attack out of fear and ridicule out of false pride.
> (*What Is the Oxford Group?*, p. 49, edited)

But there is hope, even for those of us who have practiced "contempt prior to investigation." Once we accept that some of the thoughts we have just might come from God, we are in a much better position to accept other spiritual principles which used to baffle us.

As Sam Shoemaker describes it, "We surrender as much of ourselves as we know to as much of God as we understand." For many of us, this surrender is to a God we do not understand. We are not asking you to analyze and comprehend God with your mind. Rather, we are asking you to accept God with your heart.

Now that we are willing to believe there is a God, it is time to get reconnected. This requires a complete surrender of every aspect of our lives to the Highest Power. Once we place ourselves under God's care and direction, we are no longer separated from the Spirit of the Universe.

The second question we need to ask ourselves is:

"Do I believe God can solve all of my difficulties?"

Part 3: We surrender all of our problems to God.

In order to be effective, our surrender must be complete. We need to consider turning every aspect of our lives over to God:

> Life is many-sided. How much am I willing to allow God to take control over its various interests and activities? There is my business. Is He the managing director? There is my money. Does He spend it? My time. Does He dispose of it? There are my friendships, my home, my career, my leisure. How far is God in absolute control of these?
> (*When Man Listens*, p. 18, edited)

We must not hold anything back. If we do, we will find ourselves blocked from the Voice of God:

> Are we willing to make a full surrender? To yield ourselves absolutely to God? That is the great question. What God wants is not praising lips,

reverence and prayers only—but ourselves, our powers and capacities and possessions—not a tenth of our income and one-seventh of our time, but all of our income and all of our time. The clear ringing challenge of the Group is this: are you willing to let God run your life, or will you keep it in your own hands? Are you wanting to use God for your purposes or are you willing to let Him use you for His?
(*The Eight Points of the Oxford Group*, p. 9, edited)

Willingness is the key to a successful surrender. Our minds need to be open to new ideas and perceptions. In other words, we must become teachable:

Peace, direction, power—the fullness of life—await the complete surrender of ourselves to God for His purposes. This is the great experiment that is waiting to be made—giving God control.

How do we begin this experiment?

To put it very simply, God cannot take over our lives unless we are *willing.* Willingness is not a matter of feeling. It is not a vague desire that God should change us. It is not an impulsive resolve to obey God in the future. It is a very practical thing. Something to be done right now, today.
(*When Man Listens*, p. 17, edited)

We may want reassurances that our surrender is the right thing to do. But, we can only experience the relief that comes from a complete surrender by trying it. We need to step out in faith and turn everything over to God:

The fascinating experience of getting "remade" has begun. The interest grows, because the process does not end with us. Other people notice the difference, and God begins to work in them. An area of life around us begins to change.

But how are we to be sure that this will happen? We want good reason before we take the plunge. There is only one way to be sure—by trying. It is a tremendous experiment. We only find what marriage is like by getting married. We test a remedy by taking it. That is what *faith* means. It does not mean being quite confident before-hand—working one's feelings into a state of certainty. It means making the experiment.
(*When Man Listens*, pp. 21-22, edited)

Our surrender must be complete, but it must also be ongoing. We perform a daily surrender in order to remain "in fit spiritual condition":

Surrender goes on. It is not simply an initial act. It is a process carried deeper every day. We constantly find more of ourselves to give to God. We also find more of what God can do with us. It is possible for us to give all we know of ourselves to all we know of God.
(*When Man Listens*, p. 21, edited)

Once a surrender becomes a part of our daily routine, we find it so much easier to live our lives according to God's plan rather than our own. Our little designs and schemes seem insignificant by comparison:

Our lives will be one continuous surrender:

surrender to God of every difficulty that confronts us, each temptation, each spiritual struggle; laying them before Him either to take away or to put them in their proper spiritual perspective.
(*What Is the Oxford Group?*, p. 46, edited)

A simple prayer repeated throughout the day will help keep us on the right spiritual path:

"Thy will be done" are the four little words that give us the crux to the surrender of our will-power which is usually the last thing we wish to surrender to God. Many times each day we say "Thy will be done–not mine. Thy Will shall be my will."
(*What Is the Oxford Group?*, p. 48, edited)

With practice, surrender becomes a working part of our minds. It plays a very important role when "practicing the presence of God":

Surrender is not something to be done once, but a process to be sustained, alike in mood and in action, all the way through. Indeed, it must be more than sustained; it must be continuously deepened and strengthened. Every new day must be surrendered to God. The only surrender that has value is the surrender of life in its totality. Anything consciously held back mars everything. All that is in self–the good, the bad and the indifferent–must be handed over to God. He will then give back that which is fit for us to use.
(*The Eight Points of the Oxford Group*, p. 5, edited)

Now we need to ask ourselves a third question:

"Am I willing to turn every aspect of my life over to God?"

If we can answer yes to all three questions, we are ready to make our surrender in the presence of God and another person. It is important that prayer be an integral part of the process. We will find a prayer we can use within the story that follows.

Victor Kitchen was a New York City advertising executive and member of the Calvary Church team. This was the same team that Bill Wilson, one of the co-founders of the Twelve Step Movement belonged to. In 1934, Victor wrote a book titled *I Was a Pagan.*

This book describes Victor's transformation from a selfish, self-centered materialist to a thoughtful, compassionate and effective life-changer. By all outward appearances, he is a successful man. Victor knows how to manipulate people with words. He has created a demand for various goods and services, and in the process, he has earned a great deal of money.

However, on the inside, Victor is dying. He is spiritually bankrupt. He realizes something is missing–his life is unfulfilled:

> A pagan is a person who spends time chasing false gods. And I had spent forty years of my life chasing Pleasure, Possessions, Power, Position and Praise. I now call these pagan gods my unfortunate "Five P's." One or more of them seem to have played a part in my life for as long as I could remember.
> (*I Was a Pagan*, p. 1, edited)

In the beginning, alcohol is an ally. It helps Victor succeed in his quest for the unfortunate "Five P's." But, after awhile alcohol becomes a necessity to help him cope with the futility of life as he had been living it:

> At one time, drinking seemed like an adventure. Alcohol once appeared to "make lights brighter, music sweeter, colors fairer, women more beautiful and men more companionable." But, in time I began to find that I had to drink not simply to heighten the pleasure of lights and music and the companionship of men and women but in order to stand them at all. I began to feel there might be something wrong with trudging along year after year simply to pile up as many possessions as possible, to possess a wife of whom I was growing steadily more neglectful, and to possess a thirst which gradually was ripening into insatiability. Was there nothing to look forward to except, perhaps the making of still more money, the acquisition of still more wives–perhaps some other fellow's or, perhaps, another of my own–and the drinking of still more liquor? I began to feel, that the pagan aims and purposes did not and could not represent complete success in life.
> (*I Was a Pagan*, p. 5)

Victor reaches the "jumping-off place." He realizes the futility of his efforts. His false gods have failed to provide him with either contentment or peace of mind. Remorse and self pity have replaced vanity and arrogance:

> There comes a time to almost every man when he seems to die inside, and that time came to me. I want to tell you that things looked pretty black to me right then. There seemed nothing much to do but go back to my dreary round of escapes from the home into the

office and from the office into the speakeasy.
(*I Was a Pagan*, p. 21, edited)

Then, Victor has a moment of clarity. He admits he has a problem. This is the first part of the surrender process:

Unless one is hopelessly out of touch with reality, one cannot live long under a pretense like this. One cannot go on indefinitely gilding the cabbages of life and pretending they are lilies.

My life plan could only be described as "Egotism." And since egotism had left me and most other people that I know with a great big unfilled gap in our lives–since century after century and generation after generation it had brought the world to recurring states of chaos–was it not likely that some other untried or less-tried plan would prove to be the right one? Was it not possible, for instance, that, as Einstein suggests, man's primary purpose is to help other men?
(*I Was a Pagan*, pp. 6, 12, edited)

At this point, Victor starts to contemplate a spiritual solution to his problems. He considers changing his life from self-directed to God directed. This is the second part of the surrender process–to realize that, no matter what the problem, God is the solution:

It seemed possible that the ecclesiastics might be right and that there might be some kind of an all-powerful God who created men for some purpose of His own. In that case our only real purpose in life would be to obey the will of God wherever that might lead and for whatever purpose, known or unknown.

Philosophy both past and present, seemed to
support my finding that we were living primarily to
develop a personality or soul in the life school God
provides for us. And this being so, I had not only
been bungling life but I had made an even worse mess
of it than I first supposed. Life was intended to grow
souls,   not   fortunes–to   make   character,   not
whoopee–to gain depth of understanding, not
eminence in business or social circles–to seek the will
of God, not the praise of the public.
(*I Was a Pagan*, pp. 14, 16, edited)

Victor comes to believe there is an alternative to the
materialistic, self-centered life he has been living. He sees the
value of a spiritual life based on the Four Standards of Honesty,
Purity, Unselfishness and Love:

A big man spiritually is not made up, like a big
man materially, of bank presidencies, directorships,
influence, dominance and social prestige. He is not
made up, like an intellectual giant, of doctor's degrees
and learned societies. He is made up of the simple
moral qualities of Honesty, Purity, Unselfishness and
Love. And he does not grow more honest or more
pure through increasing knowledge of what is honest
and pure. He does not "get that way" through his
intellect at all–nor through his physical prowess or
achievements.

All the material possessions I had ever acquired
and all the intellectual knowledge I had ever gathered
had not added a single cubit to my stature morally. In
fact, if anything, I had grown through the years more
dishonest, more impure, more selfish and more

unloving than ever.
(*I Was a Pagan*, pp. 21, 23, edited)

The truth has been revealed. Victor is now ready to try a different path. He becomes willing to turn his will and his life over to God:

> I had previously failed to receive this aid for the very simple reason that I had been trying to supply all the power myself–even after I learned that power for moral growth would have to come from the outside. I believed that the Lord helps those who help themselves. I was keen on self-management. I was a self-determinist, the captain of my own soul. *And this is the real secret of all human difficulty.*
>
> This sudden stepping out of the darkness is difficult–and particularly difficult for a man who does not realize that he is blind to start with. Blind fish who swim in subterranean caves cannot imagine such a thing as sunlight. Neither could the wholly selfish "blind" man that was I.
> (*I Was a Pagan*, pp. 39, 45, edited)

Self-will must be crushed if Victor is to stand in the "sunlight of the Spirit." But, he realizes he can not do this through intellectual exercises or ritualistic acts. He needs a power greater than self to overcome self–he needs the Power of God.

Victor is now ready to put his life in God's hands. This is the third part of the surrender process–making the decision to let God lead the way:

> I had put God first in theory, yet still continued to

mean well and do badly. That was because I was still
trying to run my own life. I had not put Him first in
living, but had kept my self-love uppermost and had
built my scheme of things quite upside down.

However, when I turned things around and put
God at the head of the list–when I ceased struggling
to pull myself up and stepped out of the way so that
His light could shine down to me–when I let Him
show me how to use the gifts He had given me to
accomplish for myself, for humanity and for Him, the
things He wanted me to accomplish, then, for the first
time in forty years, things of consequence began to
happen in my life.
(*I Was a Pagan*, p. 48, edited)

The Group suggests a prayer be used to complete the
surrender process. This is Victor's Surrender Prayer:

**I surrender my life to Thee, O God. Living in self
has separated me from your Divine guidance and
grace. Take my life and run it for me, according to
Your will and Your plan. Thy will, not mine be
done.**
(*I Was a Pagan*, p. 67, edited)

Once Victor completes his surrender, he realizes that his
outlook on life has changed. He is now looking at the world
through "a new pair of glasses":

It was thus that I found the "higher affection"
which my false gods, philosophies, ethics and
psychology could not supply. I came upon it not by
hearsay but through actual personal experience. I
learned to live this higher quality of life by actually

tasting the only love in the world that surpasses man's love of self and gives to him the power of regeneration.
(*I Was a Pagan*, p. 70)

Once Victor surrenders to this new "design for living," he realizes that his compulsion to drink has been removed. He has been freed from the shackles of alcohol dependence:

> After surrendering my life, I felt such peace and joy that my reciprocal, instinctive physical desire was to "celebrate as ususal" by pouring out a generous libation of alcohol. I had actually started for a bottle in the pantry when God stopped me with my first real bit of guidance and told me that I could not serve Him as long as I was a slave to gin. I then and there admitted my inability to quit of my own will and asked God to take charge of the matter. He did. I looked at the bottle and felt a distinct sensation of nausea. I was revolted at the very thought of a drink and the desire for alcohol has never come back. God simply lifted that desire entirely out of my life, and I have found this freedom far more desirable than any satisfaction or repression of desire I have ever experienced.
> (*I Was a Pagan*, pp. 73-74, edited)

Victor then addresses his other addictions and compulsions. He wants to be free of all the things that have been blocking him off from God, not just alcohol:

> Prior to this surrender, I realized that my prayers had been little but wishful thinking–that I had prayed to God chiefly to bring about the things I wanted, in

the way I wanted them to come. I then and there asked God to take over my prayer and guide it, so that I might pray for what He wanted to bring about and so that He might use me for that purpose instead of my trying to use Him.

He taught me His first great commandment–that I must love the Lord my God with all my heart and all my mind and all my soul–that, in other words, I must surrender my alcohol, my tobacco and my ladies, I must surrender my self-glorifying philosophies, and I must surrender my false gods.
(*I Was a Pagan*, pp. 82, 180, edited)

In the remaining pages of *I Was a Pagan*, Victor takes the Steps of Sharing, Restitution and Guidance. He experiences a complete spiritual transformation and becomes a life-changer. He spends the rest of his life in service to God and humanity.

This is a dramatic story of redemption and restoration. There are thousands of stories just like Victor's–stories of men and women who have overcome their afflictions, their "soul sickness," through reliance upon God and two-way prayer.

8
Step 2: Sharing

Once we have completed our Surrender, we still need to take additional Steps in order to establish and maintain a conscious contact with God. We must remove any barriers that may interfere with our communication with the Divine Inner Presence.

We can visualize this concept of two-way prayer in terms of a telephone with God at the other end of the line. One-way prayer is simply talking through the mouthpiece without putting the receiver to our ear. To hear what God has to say, we must first position the phone so we can listen.

When listening, we may hear only static. We must realize that certain characteristics of self interfere with reception. God may be there, but we can't make out what our Creator is trying to say.

The Group uses Sharing to identify the sources of the static, so they can be eliminated by Restitution. In essence, Sharing is admitting to God and to another person that we have taken certain actions based on self, which have cut us off from the the Voice within:

> Sharing means confession to God and to another
> person. It means talking freely to a "Surrendered"
> man or woman who can be trusted to keep secrets and
> to give wise counsel.
> (*For Sinners Only*, p. 25, edited)

Sharing is being honest about oneself. It demonstrates our willingness to acknowledge mistakes, admit our wrongs and take responsibility for the harm we have caused. It is a way to address the shame and guilt associated with past misdeeds so we can be free of them.

Sharing has been used as a method for healing "soul sickness" for thousands of years. The technique is not new. What the Group has done is demonstrate the importance of Sharing in simple, easy-to-understand language:

> Frank Buchman rediscovered the value of the
> spiritual prescription which James gave us, "Confess
> your faults one to another, and pray one for another
> that ye may be healed." (James 5: 16) Dr. Buchman
> prefers the more familiar word "Sharing" instead of
> confession, but the experience is the same.
> (*The Eight Points of the Oxford Group*, p. 18, edited)

Sharing rids us of the feelings and emotions that keep us living in the darkness of self-will. It is a cleansing and healing process which helps us establish and maintain a proper relationship with God:

> The ultimate aim of Sharing is a right relationship
> with God. We are in desperate need of forgiveness.
> In the last resort, whatever aids we may use to help us
> reach it, we must come to the one place where we
> stand before God face to face, confess our faults and

receive the forgiveness which God so freely gives. There is no other way to fullness of life, and in our hearts we know it.
(*For Sinners Only,* p. 26)

Sharing sets us free from the bondage of self. It helps us overcome emotional problems and physical illness:

No one will ever realize to what extent God can work through the spiritual to alleviate the troubles of the mental and physical. The Holy Spirit can give limitless power of resistance to any disease. Setting the mind free through truth can work mental and physical wonders.
(*What Is the Oxford Group?*, p. 29, edited)

We all have difficulties. Everyone has, from time to time, listened to the voice of self rather than the Voice of God. Listening to the voice that personifies self-will prevents us from maintaining a clean connection with the Spirit of the Universe:

Sharing our shortcomings brings them into the light and gives them their proper spiritual status. We acknowledge their existence and grade them according to their importance to us. These character liabilities are no longer vague shadows but hard facts to be faced squarely and in due time eradicated with God's help. No man is without faults; that is the common ground for Sharing.
(*What Is the Oxford Group?*, p. 29, edited)

We are asked to look at ourselves in a whole new light. Many of us have gone to great lengths to prove that our difficulties are due to the actions of others. We are quick to look outside rather than inside ourselves for the source of our difficulties:

> James certainly did not say "Confess other
> people's faults." There is always hope for those who
> confess their own difficulties. It is the person who
> confesses the faults of another person for whom there
> is very little hope.
> (*The Eight Points of the Oxford Group*, p. 22, edited)

The objective of Sharing is to establish and maintain two-
way prayer. Forgiveness repairs the connection so we can
obtain strength and direction directly from God:

> We cannot feel the reality of forgiveness until we
> have confessed. To many people, God is unreal. It is
> difficult for them to realize that He is always with us.
> To tell them to confess to God alone is to deprive
> them of the relief and sense of reality which Sharing
> confers.   Their solitary search for forgiveness is
> generally unsuccessful.
> (*The Eight Points of the Oxford Group*, p. 22, edited)

Here we see the necessity of sharing with another person.
The process fosters reconciliation and forgiveness:

> Ideally, confession can be made directly to God,
> without the need of human assistance. But, unfor-
> tunately, we are not ideal, and experience has shown
> the value of sharing with a "surrendered" man or
> woman, as a help toward reaching a proper
> relationship with God. Theoretically, there is no
> reason why we should not confess our faults directly
> to God and receive God's forgiveness then and there.
> Obviously, this happens time and time again. But,
> instance after instance can be quoted to show that

there are many who need the help of a sharing partner, in order to come directly face to face with God. For them sharing is a practical necessity.
(*Sharing*, pp. 4-5, edited)

Having the willingness to share with another person is a sign that we have surrendered and are prepared to go to any lengths to establish and maintain a conscious contact with God:

Once again, willingness to share with another person is an indication of true repentance. Experience shows that many go on verbally confessing the same fault to God time after time, but with no lasting victory. They have never learned the difference between mere remorse and real repentance. There are indeed cases in which the refusal to share has been the last stronghold of the pride which blocks the path to God, for there can be no life until that stronghold has fallen.
(*Sharing*, pp. 5-6, edited)

It is clear that we need to share our shortcomings with another person. But, how do we decide who is to hear our story? The Group provides some guidelines for choosing a sharing partner. First, this person must be able to keep a confidence:

Such sharing as this naturally takes place with some individual who inspires trust and a conviction that he or she can help. It is private and obviously a matter of strict confidence.
(*Sharing*, p. 6, edited)

Second, our sharing partner must have completed the Steps and be practicing two-way prayer on a daily basis:

Sharing of faults as practiced by the Group is sharing in the ordinary sense of the word. In plain language it is telling, or talking over, our shortcomings with another who has already surrendered his or her life to God.
(*What Is the Oxford Group?*, p. 27, edited)

The sharing partner is essential, because as John Batterson writes in *How to Listen to God*, "More light comes in through two windows than one":

In practice as well as in theory, sharing is very sound psychologically. "Two minds are better than one" is an old saying which is more true when the subject in discussion is common to both parties.
(*What Is the Oxford Group?*, p. 27, edited)

We have established that we need to share our faults with God and another person. Now, we need to look at what we share. The Group suggests we examine both the positive and negative characteristics of our personality. We are to conduct the equivalent of a business inventory which consists of assets and liabilities.

In *When Man Listens*, Cecil Rose writes about spiritual bankruptcy. In order to get out of debt, we have to get honest about our personal balance sheet:

If a man is bankrupt and consents to a reorganization of the business, the first thing he must do is produce the books — all of them. The difficulty with so many debtors is that they conceal some of the debts, or fail to mention some particularly foolish blunder or some doubtful transaction. A satisfactory reorganization is impossible if there is only a partial

disclosure. If we want God to take control of our lives, the first thing we must do is to produce the books. We must be willing to look, with God, at everything.
(*When Man Listens,* p. 17, edited)

It is not necessary to write this inventory, but it is helpful. We must be able to clearly document our successes and failures–the positive as well as the negative aspects of our business.

Cecil Rose took some notes as he was reviewing his books:

It may be useful at this point if I get a pencil and paper, and make some notes. This business of looking into the books is taking me further than I expected, but I must see it through.
(*When Man Listens,* p. 19)

So, Cecil took some notes. He jotted down a few items of stock that needed to be discarded and a few people to whom he needed to make restitution.

The inventory is not intended to be a long drawn out exercise in psychological futility. It is a means to an end designed to produce spiritual peace of mind through the practice of two-way prayer:

We must look at everything. We can leave no stone unturned in our quest to bring God into our lives:

The Group provides us with several lists of shortcomings that we can use for taking inventory. They consist of the characteristics of self that keep us in the dark and prevent us from listening to God:

Unhappiness for us and others, discontentment, and, frequently, mental and bodily ill health are the direct results of living on self-will. It takes no study of religious science, no contemplation of the power of thought, no extensive psychoanalysis to make us realize that. Morbidity of mind affects physical health. Our transgressions against God and our fellows can dominate us mentally and physically until we become their abject slaves. We cannot get rid of them by deciding to think no more about them; they never leave us of their own accord. Unless they are cut out by a spiritual operation which destroys them and sets us free from their killing obsession, they continue to grow, and in time we become warped in outlook not only towards others but toward ourselves. (*What Is the Oxford Group?*, p. 21, edited)

We must realize our "soul sickness" cannot be cured by the doctors and psychiatrists of the world. We cannot overcome self by relying on self. Our objective is not to understand the mind, but rather to set the mind free of the anger, fear, resentment and shame that have been preventing us from realizing our God given potential:

Pathological psychology has become fashionable in recent years. The subconscious has been elevated to a position of prominence. It is supposed to rule our destinies and be at the root of all we think, say or do. Any failing or abnormality, however hideous, can be blamed on our subconscious mind, which has become a gold mine for those who seek to profit by the frailties of human nature. (*What Is the Oxford Group?*, p. 19, edited)

This is the feeble "But, it's not my fault" response to our

difficulties. In the Group we learn to take responsibility for our actions and to stop blaming others for our shortcomings:

> Living on self-will is called by the modern intelligentsia by any name but it's own. To these "highbrows" our transgressions are repressed desires; inhibitions; fixations; morbid introspection; suppression of natural instincts and other words ending in "ism," "phobia," "mania"–anything but what they are–characteristics of self which have blocked us off from God.
> (*What Is the Oxford Group?*, p. 20, edited)

Let us take a look at what we have to do in order to learn the truth about ourselves. We are born with a direct link to our Creator. It is time to get reconnected. We need to conduct the equivalent of a business inventory on our lives. We look at our liabilities in order to remove those things which have been blocking us.

The assets side of the ledger consists of the Four Standards. These positive characteristics of our personalities have been described in detail in a previous chapter. The source of the Four Standards is described by Cecil Rose in *When Man Listens*:

> A good way to begin this examination of the books is to test our lives beside the Sermon on the Mount. A convenient and pointed summary of its teaching has been made under the four headings of Honesty, Purity, Unselfishness and Love.
> (*When Man Listens*, p. 18, edited)

Several Group authors describe the liabilities side of the ledger. Hugh Redwood, who wrote *God in the Slums*, graphically explains the dark side of our character:

There are slums other than those which sprawl in our modern cities. These are slums within the human soul. They flourish in every rank of society and every type of person.

Dishonesty, Lust, Violence and Hatred are open menaces, but these cellars of the soul often lie concealed in the lives of good and religious people. In addition, there are the slums of Resentment, Self-righteousness and Criticism which are difficult to clean up because the tenants have such intense pride of ownership. Independence, Prejudice and False Pride seem to be handsome structures, but many families and friends are sacrificed to pay the mortgage on them. Jealousy has a high picket fence where love and friendship are often impaled and die bleeding. The night cries of Fear disturb the peace of these neighborhoods; fear of being found out, fear of people, fear of the future, fear of ill-health, fear of failure, fear of death. Selfishness hangs like a choking fog over everything, and a very foul drainage system called Gossip runs from tenement to tenement. (*The Guidance of God*, pp. 12-14, edited)

In this short paragraph, Hugh Redwood lists fourteen liabilities. In addition he names six forms of fear.

Victor Kitchen, in his book titled *I Was a Pagan*, also describes an assets and liabilities checklist. On the liabilities side of the ledger he lists eight attributes of self-will.

In *For Sinners Only*, A. J. Russell gives us a detailed look at the liabilities side of the ledger. He presents four general categories of negative attributes which are grouped into categories which correspond to the opposites of the Four Standards. We will describe each of the liabilities on this list and summarize them into an assets and liabilities checklist we can use as a guide for Sharing:

> Liabilities are those thoughts, words or actions that are contrary to the will of God. There is no complete catalogue of these shortcomings, since what is "sin to one might not always be sin to another." But, some transgressions appear to be generally accepted by most societies. They are drunkenness, false pride, murder, dishonesty, selfishness, refusal to love God or one's neighbor, and coveting another man's wife or loving the husband of another woman. Others we can add to this list are overeating, vain boasting, laziness, gambling, wasting money in nightclubs, and refusing to trust God at all times. We might include making fun of someone who is poorly dressed and lying about the time we left the office, what we owed the butcher or how much we lost at cards. Also, being unwilling to play the Good Samaritan to a broken-down motorist or a weary older person on the subway can be included, as can graft, greed, belligerence, fear, waste, meanness, aversion and perversion. All of these and many others can be considered to be manifestations of self which separate us from God.
> (*For Sinners Only*, p. 61, edited)

On the liabilities side of the leger, A. J. Russell lists four major headings. They are Dishonesty, Impurity, Fear and Selfishness. We will now examine each of these categories.

Dishonesty

Dishonesty can be divided into the two subcategories of "sins of the tongue" (falsehood) and "stealing" (theft):

Falsehood
First is **misstatement** or **misrepresentation,** by exaggerating or minimizing or giving a false emphasis, usually for our own glory.

Second is **concealment** and **dishonest silences.**

Third, we evade by the simple device of **polite lying and false excuses.** It is "politically correct" to call a behavior an "inferiority complex," when, in reality, it is a very simple but deadly form of false pride.

Fourth, there is **criticism** which is faultfinding or a negative judgment about people or their work.

Fifth, it is easy to slip into **double-dealing** which is saying one thing to a person's face and another thing behind his or her back.
(*For Sinners Only*, p. 320, edited)

Theft
Then there is the matter of **stealing,** which consists of taking someone else's property without their consent. It includes stealing from companies as well as from individuals. Examples of the former include traveling first-class with a third-class ticket or entering a football game by the cheap entrance and going under the ropes to the more expensive section.
(*For Sinners Only*, p. 320, edited)

Impurity

Impurity of thought and deed has to do with fantasies and actions which are outside the accepted mores of a society. Because each culture has its own set of values, it is important to understand and be tolerant of other people's beliefs. There is no universal set of values. Rather, there are some general principles which can guide us in terms of what is right and what is wrong.

Impurity of thought covers our secret desires:

> Moral impurity begins with the eye and the thought. How would you feel if your thought-life were suddenly thrown upon a screen for everyone to see?

> We also need to deal with the tongue and the touch. For many of us our history is this: the look, the thought, the fascination and then the fall. With regard to our relationships with the opposite sex, there may be fellowship but there must never be familiarity.
> (*For Sinners Only*, p. 322, edited)

Selfishness

Selfishness can manifest itself in many ways. Some of these are False Pride, Envy, Jealousy, Laziness, Prejudice and Self-centeredness.

False pride is a two-edged sword. It injures us as well as others when we think we are less than or better than our fellows:

False Pride

There are many different forms in which false pride operates in our lives. Self-love shows itself in the love of praise and popularity and social success. Often we stand on what we are pleased to call our dignity. In fact, our dignity is so well stood on that there's really not much left.

We dread almost more than anything to make a fool of ourselves. We develop what we are pleased to call sensitiveness, but which we can better call touchiness. Then self-pity creeps in. We feel inferior. We positively hug failure and point to previous defeats as evidence of our limitations. Or we may develop a martyr complex with all its false heroics. (*For Sinners Only*, p. 324, edited)

Two other manifestations of selfishness, envy and jealousy, are closely related. Envy has to do with possessions, and jealousy has to do with relationships:

Envy

Self-interest about money or possessions shows itself by our unwillingness to lend or give our things to others. We spend too much time thinking about possessions, both ours and those belonging to our fellows. We suffer from an exaggerated carefulness about our belongings. It makes us preoccupied and worried with our own affairs. We become "penny wise and pound foolish."
(*For Sinners Only*, p. 324-325, edited)

Jealousy

Jealousy is devastating to peace of mind and spiritual power. Self importance often gives rise to

jealousy. We demand complete devotion from others and we become suspicious of those whom we think have an advantage over us.
(*For Sinners Only*, pp. 323-324, edited)

Laziness is more than just idleness. It includes procrastination, which involves putting off what should be done and chronic lateness, which shows a lack of interest in or indifference toward others:

Laziness

One of the most common forms of selfishness is self-indulgence. There is self-indulgence in food and physical comforts. But we also indulge ourselves when we are lazy or procrastinate, or when we are unpunctual. We say we'll put off until tomorrow that which we should have done yesterday.
(*For Sinners Only*, p. 325, edited)

Opinions of others based solely on race, color or creed constitutes prejudice. It is an extreme form of false pride–a feeling we are better than someone else just because of the color of our skin or the church we attend:

Prejudice

We often have no hesitation in being rude to people we may not like or whom we consider socially inferior. We indulge ourselves by airing our bias about people, airing our likes and dislikes in matters of books, food, furniture and furnishings. We are tremendously taken up with whether a person meets our standards.
(*For Sinners Only*, pp. 325-326)

Self-centeredness is all about maintaining the illusion that the world revolves about us. It includes unprincipled ambition–wanting our own way, no matter what the consequences or the cost:

Self-centeredness

Self-centeredness reveals a life where we are still rotating about the axis of ego. There is the need for self-display which shows itself in the love of the spotlight and the love of attention. We love our opinions and we are ready to assert them, even though we may know very little about the subject.

We simply want our own way, and we will not yield. The results are as obvious as they are disastrous. It brings friction with others and frustration for us. We do not know the meaning of teamwork. Consequently, we are useless to the people and the situations around us. With our self-will unchecked we become trying in our actions, unguided in our decisions, demanding in our efforts and impatient of others.

We get caught up in ambition which disregards the interest of others and is unscrupulous about the methods used to reach financial or career goals. It leads to false objectives in self-chosen service. The results, which ought to accompany the working of the Holy Spirit, are manifestly absent. This leads to false activity to cover up an inward sense of dissatisfaction, futility and frustration, which haunts all of us when our lives are run on self-effort.

We feel we do not need anyone else's help. This is the result of too small a conception of God and too large a conception of our own capacities.
(*For Sinners Only*, pp. 325-327, edited)

Fear

Fear can be overwhelming and debilitating. It distorts our perception of reality and leaves us in an anxious state of immobilization. When we find ourselves irritated, depressed, angry or ill, we can be sure fear is at the source.

We erroneously believe that the fears of the past can successfully predict the fears of the future. As a result, we spend most of our time worrying about both the past and the future, creating a vicious cycle of fear, which leaves little room for living in the present.

Fear and Love are mutually exclusive emotions. They cannot be experienced at the same time. In the final analysis, it is our choice as to which of these emotions we project upon those around us.

Fear can materialize in many different forms. It prevents us from feeling the love that surrounds us every day:

> The sin of Fear is a sin against love. Perfect love conquers fear. Most of us are afraid of others and consequently we can't feel comfortable around them. (*For Sinners Only*, p. 324, edited)

The manifestations of fear are hatred, criticism, resentment and anger. We use these emotions to cover our fear of losing something we have or not getting something we want:

Hatred
The major religions of the world tell us that hate is equivalent to murder. The one is as bad as the other. Is there anyone for whom you still harbor feelings of displeasure, disapproval or lack of

forgiveness? The issue is fairly serious.
(*For Sinners Only*, p. 322, edited)

Criticism

Criticism often hides much ill-will. Remember, we criticize in others what's wrong in ourselves. We reveal our true selves by our fault finding, our denunciations and our prejudices. *Only say about others what you say to others.*
(*For Sinners Only*, p. 323, edited)

Resentment

When we disapprove of or are annoyed by another person's point of view or their weaknesses we are demonstrating a devastating form of lovelessness. Resentment makes us irrational and separates us from others.
(*For Sinners Only*, p. 323, edited)

Anger

Rage, fury and violence are all part of an ill temper which separates us from love. Have you apologized for the last time you lost your temper with someone, with a member of your own family, a bus conductor or a railway clerk?
(*For Sinners Only*, p. 323, edited)

This list of assets and liabilities can be summarized as follows:

Liabilities	Assets
Dishonesty	Honesty
Falsehood	
Theft	
Impurity	Purity
Thought	
Deed	
Selfishness	Unselfishness
False Pride	
Jealousy	
Envy	
Ambition	
Laziness	
Prejudice	
Self-centeredness	
Fear	Love
Hatred	
Criticism	
Resentment	
Anger	

We use these shortcomings as a means to compensate for our lack of power. It is only when we make the transition from a life run on self-will to a life guided by God's will, do we receive the Power we have been so desperately seeking:

> These are some of our alternatives to a God centered and God controlled life. We seek compensation for our defeat and for our lack of power. We need anesthetics to stop the pain and discomfort, and to help us forget. We play with alternatives rather

than asking God to help us. We adopt camouflage to cover up our defects and to hide from one another. (*For Sinners Only*, pp. 328-329, edited)

So, now we have the tools to conduct a thorough inventory of our assets and liabilities. Many find it convenient to take a piece of paper and list assets on one side with liabilities on the other. We review our thoughts, words and actions, and we check the liabilities that apply. We review this list with our sharing partner and determine where we need to make restitution for any damage or harm we may have brought about because of our selfishness.

Now, it is time to break through the barriers that separate us from God and our fellows. We do this by turning our shortcomings over to God so they can be forgiven once and for all. In essence, we make a second surrender. We give to God all the characteristics of self which we have found to be objectionable:

> These, then, are the elements of spiritual transformation: surrender of our lives to God, honest and thorough facing of ourselves, restitution to others, and guidance as the result of obedience. They are best talked through with another person. It is easy to deceive ourselves, to escape the real shame and humiliation of our transgressions, or to evade the necessary steps. To face a completely honest talk with someone we can trust makes us see ourselves as we could never do in any other way. It may bring to light much that we have missed. It will certainly make it harder for us to go back or postpone carrying out our resolutions. This is one of the purposes for which God has given us fellowship. It is dangerous to neglect it.

(*When Man Listens*, p. 20, edited)

Once we have completed an assets and liabilities checklist, shared it with another person, and turned our shortcomings over to God, we will be rewarded:

> The Group insists on the power of Sharing to fill the spirit with an entirely new sense of life. And this is not at all mysterious. Sharing comes of a willingness to be absolutely honest about oneself; it is a sign that the long attempt to compromise is over, an indication that the personality is no longer divided within itself, an evidence that the soul really means what it says. When we are honest with God, with ourselves and with other people, we are born again. (*The Eight Points of the Oxford Group*, p. 20, edited)

These rewards can be described as a series of promises which will come true for us if we are willing to do the work necessary to identify and eliminate our shortcomings:

> This surrender, if it is thorough and honest, is met at once from God's side. When we hand over, God takes charge, and things begin to happen. A world of strain falls from us. The business of running life is off our hands. We find that we get through more work, because it is being ordered better. We meet people we were afraid of, and discover that fear has gone. A habit that always beat us seems to have lost its power. Someone we could not bear appears to us in a new light, and we love them. We come through an ordeal and know that it was not in our own strength.
> (*When Man Listens*, p. 21)

Victor Kitchen describes how he went through the Sharing process. He examines both his assets and liabilities, discusses them with another person, and then turns them over to God. First, he realizes that self is the source of his problems:

> I found that self crept into almost everything I had done . Whether insidious or gross, this selfishness had shut me off from a true consciousness of God.
> (*I Was a Pagan*, p. 46, edited)

Victor sees himself as spiritually blind. He needs to "consider the plank in his own eye":

> It is difficult to explain colors to a man who is color blind. Moral blindness is much the same thing, and it is a blindness which can be cleared away only when one becomes sensitive to the light of the spiritual realm.
>
> In ordinary terms, therefore, I can only say that I had been unable to see light because I stood in my own way. Powerful as the light of God is, man's own shadow will blot it out of consciousness. God cannot be heard in a mind busy with other and coarser matters.
> (*I Was a Pagan*, p. 42, edited)

Victor makes a list of his assets and liabilities. He reviews his conduct to determine what items have kept him living in the darkness and what items will help him enter the "sunlight of the Spirit":

> I felt that my character possessed many negative attributes such as fear, anger, revenge and pride; and

that it also held many positive potentialities such as poise, good nature, sympathy and understanding. I tried to make a chart of these things, showing which qualities fell on the positive side and which on the negative.
(I Was a Pagan, p. 6)

He discusses his list with his sharing partner and, in the process, discovers a new way of living. He overcomes the selfish, self-centered five P's of Pleasure, Possessions, Power, Position and Praise, and substitutes five new P's for them:

Among the P's I had turned to in life, it was my partner who came through in the pinch and put me on the track of five new P's–the Peace, Plenty, Purpose, Progress and new form of Power I had never known.
(*I Was a Pagan*, p. 50, edited)

Victor surrenders his shortcomings to God and enters into a new relationship with his Creator:

Spiritual growth, however, was far more than a matter of clearing the vision. I not only could see new things in life but began to do new things–to find new forms of happiness for myself and to enter into new forms of usefulness for man and God.
(*I Was a Pagan*, p. 168, edited)

Just like Victor, we are all well on our way to experiencing "a new freedom and a new happiness." All we need to do is use the assets and liabilities checklist as a guide and conduct the equivalent of a business inventory on our lives. With a sharing partner, discuss the shortcomings that apply and together determine where restitution or forgiveness is needed that will clear the static from the line between us, God and our fellows:

> This calls for a very considerable change–from a
> nature ruled by lust, selfishness, jealousy and hate, to
> a nature lit up by love, charity and kindness.
> (*I Was a Pagan*, p. 32, edited)

Remember that spiritual growth is in the Sharing rather than in the writing. Taking some notes during the sharing process helps us focus on what is bothering us and what we must do to right the wrongs. It also helps us to see the assets we have and those that will be enhanced as we make an amends for each of our shortcomings:

> This sensation of release and freedom is an almost
> universal experience for all who face and confess their
> faults under the eyes of God and one other person.
> (*I Was a Pagan*, p. 66, edited)

Now is the time to clear away the wreckage of the past and begin to walk "hand in hand with the Spirit of the Universe." There is no right or wrong way to take inventory and evaluate "the stock in trade." Just do it.

Assets and Liabilities Checklist

Liabilities Watch for—														Assets Strive for—
Dishonesty														Honesty
Falsehood														
Theft														
Impurity														Purity
Thought														
Deed														
Selfishness														Unselfishness
False Pride														
Envy														
Jealousy														
Laziness														
Prejudice														
Self-Centeredness														
Fear														Love
Hatred														
Criticism														
Resentment														
Anger														

James Houck shares guidance with one of the Syracuse, NY team members (at the Syracuse airport following a weekend seminar on two-way prayer)

Once-a-week Guidance Meetings and informal, one-on-one sharing sessions have been established throughout the world as the direct result of James Houck reintroducing the "How to Listen to God" pamphlet in 1996

9

Step 3: Restitution

Many of those who have had their lives changed in the past four years refer to James Houck as "Mr. Restitution." James is a firm believer in using the amends process to become a life-changer. Miraculous events have come to pass in his own life and in the lives of thousands of others who have made restitution an integral part of their spiritual journey. James describes restitution in terms of "converting barriers to bridges."

In the previous chapter, we identified those aspects of self which have kept us separated from God. Now, it is time to clean the slate–to right the wrongs–by going to those we have harmed and making amends. Restitution moves us from the liabilities to the assets side of the checklist. In addition, it provides us with the opportunity to help those who are in need of a spiritual solution to their "soul sickness."

Restitution is defined as returning something to a former or original state. For us, it eliminates the static on the telephone line between us and God and reestablishes a clear channel for effective communication.

In Chapter Eleven we will learn how to change other

people's lives by taking them through the Five C's of Confidence, Confession, Conviction, Conversion and Continuance. In this Chapter, we will describe the method for changing others by making amends to them.

We rely upon God to lead us through the restitution process. If we are unwilling to proceed, we will remain separated from the source of all power. We are right back where we started, relying upon self-will alone to solve our problems. Since self-will has gotten us into trouble in the first place, it is best to move forward into the "sunlight of the Spirit" rather than remain trapped in the cold and lonely shadows of the past.

When making amends, we find that the people we approach usually respond in one of three ways. They will either accept or reject our amends or ask us to explain what is going on.

If a person accepts the amends, we can then discuss the means of restitution. If he or she wants to know more, we have an opportunity to secure that person's confidence and trust. If the person rejects our amends, we have still completed our primary task which is to clear away the static which has separated us from God. In addition, we may have planted a spiritual seed. With proper care and nourishment, this seed can blossom into a changed life in the future.

If the person we have approached wants to continue the conversation, we have converted the barrier between us to a bridge. What was a vertical barrier becomes a horizontal plane. If the person opens up to us, we have converted the barrier into a two-way bridge. Once a two-way bridge has been established, we are able to communicate the truth about our previous life, declare that we have changed, and demonstrate our willingness to straighten out the past. When we do this, Divine Guidance can flow between us.

In *What Is the Oxford Group?*, the author provides us with an overview of the restitution process:

> Restitution is openly cutting the chains of selfish self-centeredness which have bound us to a life of wrong thinking and wrong doing. The only way of doing this is to acknowledge our faults to the people concerned and to pay back by apology or in kind that which we have taken from them.
> (*What Is the Oxford Group?*, p. 55, edited)

Without Restitution, we cannot get reconnected to God. We must right the wrongs if we are to overcome our difficulties:

> We cannot make effective contact with God while our hearts are choked with resentments. Sharing enables us to test our conduct by God's will for us and others. Restitution redeems us from blindness, listlessness and self concern, and it gives us new insight into our obligations to God's other children.
>
> Restitution is a very important principle. It is of little use to surrender our lives to God and attempt to live a changed life, if we cannot get honest about our wrong thoughts and actions in connection with those we love, work with, or come in contact with in our daily lives.
> (*The Eight Points of the Oxford Group*, pp. 31, 38, edited)

All that is required to make good on our past misdeeds is the willingness to proceed. Restitution takes courage; God will provide all the courage we need to see us through the ordeal of Restitution:

> Next, I must be willing to take any steps which God shows me, to right the wrongs I have done. There may be a broken relationship to be healed, an apology to be offered, a sin to be confessed to the person most concerned, or reparations to be made for some dishonesty.
> (*When Man Listens*, p. 19, edited)

If we let God guide us through the Restitution process, we will find it much easier than we ever thought possible. Situations which seemed beyond our ability to make right are taken care of in ways we never could have imagined or planned on our own:

> Restitution is not easy. Only those who have done so realize the strength that is required to write a letter of restitution to a person thousands of miles away, even though that transgression may be known only to the writer. But, we realize that God is with us and that restitution is necessary. As a result, our hand will be guided by God as we approach the postal box and put the letter beyond our reach and carry out one more act of atonement that will set us free from our past selves.
> (*What Is the Oxford Group?*, p. 58, edited)

Sometimes when fear sets in, we end up making excuses rather than amends. We must realize we are not making restitution only for ourselves. We are there to be of service to those we have harmed, knowing that someone we are about to approach is in need of our help:

Sometimes our pride sneaks back in and provides us with what appear to be good excuses for not making atonement for some wrong which may lie hidden from man but not from God. If we can get honest with ourselves and overcome our pride, we will realize that restitution is absolutely necessary, whatever the cost, if we are to right an injustice to another and put ourselves right with God.
(*What Is the Oxford Group?*, p. 61, edited)

What if we believe we are going to cause more harm than good by making an amends? This can be just another excuse–a way of rationalizing our way out of making restitution.

It is not up to us to decide who we are to make amends to–it is up to God. The key is to let God lead us through the process:

"What if my restitution towards a certain person does more harm than good?" Some of us, seemingly with good excuse, often ask that. The answer is that, where it is essential, the important thing for us is to go through with the restitution, for none of us knows for certain what effects our amends will have until after we have made them.

Into this problem enters the important solution of God-guidance. If we remember that surrendered lives are in truth God-directed lives, prayer can help us where we cannot help ourselves. We are often inclined to forget that God can take care of other people even better than we can.
(*What Is the Oxford Group?*, pp. 61-62, edited)

We must use discretion when we make an amends. This is

where a sharing partner can be very helpful. Where two or more are gathered together in God's name, great events will come to pass. This is the case even when it comes to the difficult task of making an amends.

Before we proceed, we ask God for guidance on how best to approach each individual and for the strength to carry through with our desire to set each matter straight. As we invite God into our lives, we begin to receive the power and direction we need to accomplish our objective:

> It is of no profit to God or man for us to wreck innocent lives by indiscretions prompted by over zealous amends. We must rely upon the discretion of the Holy Spirit. God-given guidance should be the driving force behind all our acts of restitution, telling us what to say, and when to say it and giving us, if we need it, the spiritual strength to carry them out for the best for all parties concerned.
> (*What Is the Oxford Group?*, p. 62, edited)

But, what about the people who have harmed us? Is there anything we can do to right the wrong in this situation? Yes, there is. We can forgive them.

Even though there are no amends or restitutions to be made, there is work to be done. If we harbor resentment or fear over a past abuse or affront to us, we are still blocked off from God. As a part of our restitution, we not only make an amends to those we have harmed but we also forgive those who have harmed us. Forgiveness for the wrongs of others elevates us to the "spiritual high ground":

> It takes two to make a quarrel, but one can always end it. A more glorious victory cannot be

gained over another person than to be kind and loving in spite of an injury that began on his or her part. One of the most prolific sources of human misery lies in the spirit that harbors grudges for wrongs inflicted.
(*The Eight Points of the Oxford Group*, p. 32)

To forgive others for their harms is the ultimate display of unselfishness. Forgiveness moves us closer to God–the source of all absolution and grace:

> Forgiveness is not a luxury, but an inescapable necessity. "Agree with thine adversary quickly"–quickly so that animosities will not have time to grow. Settle your differences before you separate or a difference becomes a hatred and a hatred a passion for revenge. Nurse a grievance and it grows like Jack's beanstalk. Half a day's steady thinking upon some slight makes it appear one of the greatest crimes of the century. Once we have formed a habit of nursing grievances we shall never lack one to nurse. There will always be someone to injure us, offend us and betray us.
> (*The Eight Points of the Oxford Group*, p. 32, edited)

Forgiveness is also a demonstration of unconditional love. By reaching out to someone who is selfish and self-serving, we have the opportunity to release them from their prison of loneliness and guilt, so they, too, can know the true meaning of freedom and happiness:

> "I say unto you, forgive your enemies." It is the only practical solution. No other method works.
>
> Vindictiveness does not succeed. It cannot

succeed. Trying to cure evil with evil is as futile as
trying to put out a fire with kerosene.

> Anger is a waste of energy and vitality. If we
> allow others to upset us, they end up poisoning our
> minds, disturbing our sleep and destroying our
> spiritual life.
> (*The Eight Points of the Oxford Group*, p. 33, edited)

Forgiveness is a difficult part of the restitution process.
Nobody said it would be easy. It just has to be done:

> Distressing things happen to most of us–venom-
> ous attacks which seem hardly explicable save on the
> theory that everybody is mad at some point.
> Forgiveness is not easy. A deep personal wrong
> wounds and stings. But for our own sakes we must
> not harbor thoughts of revenge. If we are the injured
> party we must take the initiative because we are in the
> stronger position. Our innocence is our strength.
> (*The Eight Points of the Oxford Group*, p. 34, edited)

We draw closer to God each time we forgive another for
their transgressions. God loves all of us–even those who have
turned their back on God and are living inappropriately. We
become more God-like when we act as God would have us. We
assume our rightful place in God's Universe–a blessed child of
the omnipresent Father:

> If I keep forgiveness within my heart and fail to
> give it expression, it perishes. I must go out and share
> that forgiveness with those who have spoken ill of me,
> slandered me, and spitefully used me, if I am to retain
> the sense of God's forgiveness. I must not shut the
> door against God and make it impossible for Him to

bestow peace and tranquility upon my spirit. Resentment and revenge are cheap and conventional but forgiveness is constructive and Godlike. We need not be afraid of forgiveness–it is powerful grace which never fails, whereas retaliation is a poor, weak act which never succeeds.
(*The Eight Points of the Oxford Group*, p. 35, edited)

Restitution is also a method for changing other peoples' lives. We are now living a God directed life. One of the best ways we can be of service to God is to bring the concept of two-way prayer to those in need.

Although making Restitution can be difficult and distressing, it becomes much easier when we think in terms of helping others. It is not about us anymore–it is about changing lives:

Restitution is righting, to the best of our present ability, the wrongs we have committed in the past. Often when we honestly and frankly acknowledge a transgression to the person we have wronged, that person is awakened to the realization of what a Changed Life can mean to him or her. Our act of restitution not only brings forgiveness, but it also brings a new life to God.
(*What Is the Oxford Group?*, p. 56, edited)

When making amends, we confess the liability that has caused the friction or discord. We tell the person we must do this in order to be free of it. The transgression has been interfering with our peace of mind and we need to set the record straight.

Approached in such a way, most people will react with compassion and understanding. They may even want to know what has caused our change of heart.

When those whom we have harmed want to know more about our reason for coming to them, they are in effect, giving us permission to proceed. We can then go into the details of what we have done and how we propose to correct the injustice or injury.

If they are curious as to why we are making an amends to them at this time, we tell them of our new discovery–a way of living based on the strength, direction and guidance of God:

> Whenever reasonably possible one should not only confess to the person we have wronged, but make restitution. Distasteful though this teaching is, it has a strong appeal to the highest spirits, and has often been used to change the lives of those confessed to as well as the lives of those who confessed.
> (*For Sinners Only,* pp. 63-64, edited)

We must be sure our motives are pure when we make our amends. We are there to help them as we clean up our side of the street. We are not there to feed our own ego by trying to make them feel sorry for us:

> Restitution should only be made under guidance with a view to helping the people concerned. Don't make restitution for your own amusement. There are people in the world who are spiritual Pharisees, who make restitution for the sake of working off an emotional complex. These people are not helping others but rather they are using others for their own selfish ends. In the Group, a person may ask guidance from other members of the team, but in principle he or she must decide how best to proceed. The rule in these matters of difficulty is to get at the real motive.
> (*For Sinners Only,* p. 286, edited)

In the process of making restitution, not all barriers will be converted to bridges. In the cases where our attempt at Restitution is rebuffed or rejected, the best we can hope for is to plant a seed of reconciliation. Sometimes this seed will germinate months or even years after the amends is attempted:

> We must not expect all our acts of restitution to be received with acclamations of joy as if we are all prodigal sons returning home. Our amends may be flatly ignored. But, if we make our restitution in the right spirit, it is certain that we shall know the power of God as an inward reality.
>
> (*What Is the Oxford Group?*, p. 64, edited)

Testimonials of the miraculous events that have come to pass as the direct result of Restitution can be found throughout the Group literature. In *For Sinners Only*, A. J. Russell writes about some of his restitution experiences. One incident involves Cleve Hicks, a Group life-changer and personal friend of James Houck. James has remarked that Cleve was the greatest life-changer he had ever met. That is saying something, coming from a man who has changed hundreds of thousands of lives himself.

Cleve was a Harvard University Chaplain with a great sense of humor. He had a very basic, down-to-earth approach to life changing:

> A man of sixty-five, when confronted with the Group teaching on the subject of Restitution, told Reverend Hicks it would take him the rest of his life to straighten out all the crooked things he had done. Cleve cheerfully replied that he could not embark on a more useful undertaking.
>
> (*For Sinners Only*, p. 129, edited)

A high school student, in relating his story of Restitution, tells how Cleve played a key role in his transformation:

> When we got to the Group meeting who should we bump into but Cleve Hicks! The next night up in Cleve's hotel room we surrendered our lives to God.
>
> Well, I "took off" and made amends to my friends for all the lies I had told them. I humbled myself to the school principal, and in so doing told him I had found a new way of living. He was in a hurry to be about his business, but when he found out I had asked God to run my life, he took the time to give me a talk on keeping up the good work. When he finished, I thanked him and walked out, saying to myself, "Well, isn't that funny–making a friend of somebody I never liked until today?"
>
> He wasn't the only friend I made. I confessed to everyone I could recall telling a lie to, thereby making friends out of enemies. I took back to the football coach some equipment I had stolen, and straightened out the misgivings I had toward some girls I had tried to take advantage of. I have also been used by God to win others to this new way of life.
> (*For Sinners Only*, p. 132, edited)

What an amazing story of conversion and life-changing! And to think, this person was only a teenager when he turned his will and his life over to God.

In *For Sinners Only*, A. J. Russell relates his personal experiences with Restitution. When he approaches someone to whom he has been dishonest, A. J., not only has his debt forgiven, but he received a financial gift greater than the amount for which he was making an amends:

> That evening I had to do a little more restitution. I had been tutoring a son of a rich man for a considerable sum of money on an out-of-date teaching certificate. I was guided to tell the man the truth about this, and stood to lose everything I had earned. Instead of losing anything, I found a new friend. The man was very pleasant. He not only rehired me for the summer, but he donated an amount of money equal to all my past wages to the Group's South African venture as well.
> (*For Sinners Only*, p. 105)

On these pages, we have been following the spiritual transformation of Victor Kitchen. Up to this point, Victor has made his Surrender and has been Sharing his character liabilities with his sharing partner. Now he is about to sweep off his side of the street and, in the process, change lives:

> With the help of God, I overcame my laziness. Where I used to drag myself out of bed somewhere between eight and ten in the morning, it is seldom now that I am not up by five or six, eager to spend an hour alone with God and start the day right, under his guidance. And, where, I used to halfheartedly give eight hours a day to my business, I now quite often put in eighteen hours at the work God directs me to do.
> (*I Was a Pagan*, p. 74, edited)

When taking inventory, Victor realizes he has been unable to get close to his sister because of his false pride. This shortcoming has prevented him from being of help to her:

> I sincerely wanted to help my own sister, but did not want to let her or others see that I had no real answer

for her problems. Like the would-be-helpers who have
nothing but a ton of coal to give the poor, I had nothing
but a tome of philosophy to give her. To cover up this
lack of compassion, I started "talking down" to her,
pretending to be on a level I had never myself attained.
Nobody, naturally, was helped–least of all my sister.
(*I Was a Pagan*, p. 76, edited)

When Victor makes an amends for his shortcomings, his sister
immediately realizes that his life has changed. The vertical barrier
between them becomes a horizontal bridge:

By making amends to my sister, I was able to enter
immediately into a new and vital relationship with her.
I could now give the kind of help that neither a ton of
coal nor a tome of philosophy had ever brought to
anyone. My sister, whom I had mistreated for so long,
was the first person God enabled me to help by this new
quality of life. The first letter after my change brought a
surprised and delighted response from her. "What has
happened to you?" she wrote. "I feel something is
different between us. For the first time in your life you
seem to be helping me."
(*I Was a Pagan*, pp. 76-77, edited)

Victor explains how he was able to change his relationship
with his wife by making Restitution. In this case, false pride was
again the culprit:

Even before I was married, I had decided to
"reform" my future wife. I decided, among many other
changes obviously needed, that I would "bring her up to
my intellectual level" in order that she might become an
intelligent and complementary sounding board for my
philosophical discourses. Once, however, she fell asleep

as I was reading aloud to her a volume on the history of civilization. I then decided to abandon the attempt to change her and spend my later years merely pointing out her faults.
(*I Was a Pagan*, p. 85, edited)

Constant criticism became Victor's way of trying to remain in control of the marital relationship. He spent a considerable amount of time telling her how much better off they would both be if she would just do things his way:

> She should, I told her, speak less sharply to the children. She should prove less diligent in inventing tiresome errands for me to do. She should spend less money on practically everything and keep the children from pounding on the piano and playing the radio too loudly. Everything I was sure would turn out much better if she would correct her erroneous ways. And everything would have been much better–for my ego.
> (*I Was a Pagan*, pp. 85-86, edited)

Victor finally sees the futility of life as he has been living it. Instead of continuing to blame his wife for all his problems, Victor starts to look within himself. He sees where he has been at fault and makes an amends. Victor's adversarial wife becomes his sharing partner:

> Here, I think, has been my most conspicuous re-direction. I see now the utter futility of trying to reform my wife without starting to reform myself. I no longer tell my wife to check her tongue. Because God is directing and empowering me, I instead check my own. When I find myself speaking sharply, I realize that I have amends to make. I used to be too preoccupied with myself to seek guidance on matters having to do with

the two of us. I now sit down with her and together we work out our differences.
(*I Was a Pagan*, p. 87, edited)

Victor also makes Restitution at work. He initially thinks he will be ruined if he becomes honest with his clients and with the public:

I first drew back from the Group's challenge and told them it would be utterly impossible to start being honest in the advertising business. That was an evasion. In actuality, I meant that it would be difficult, embarrassing and probably unprofitable. God showed me, however, that it was not only possible to be honest in advertising, but it was also possible to be unselfish, loving and pure.
(*I Was a Pagan*, p. 120, edited)

Victor makes a financial amends to his partner and the very next day receives guidance on how to become an honest advertising agent. When Victor listens, God guides him to a more profitable as well as more honorable way of doing business:

On my first day back to work, God gave me courage to hand my partner a check for the estimated discrepancy in my expense account. The next day God guided me to open a magazine I seldom read and turn directly to a page and paragraph which gave me the directions as to how I could be wholly honest in the advertising I wrote.
(*I Was a Pagan*, p. 120, edited)

Victor summarizes his Restitution experience with the following statement:

I let God remove the obstacles that had kept His love from flowing in.
(*I Was a Pagan*, p. 180, edited)

By making restitution, we remove the characteristics of self which keep us blocked from God:

These stories of reconciliation and restitution all point to new principles at work in the lives of the people involved in this life-changing work. They are examples of the quality of life which this movement is trying to achieve.
(*For Sinners Only*, p. 134)

So, now it is time to clear away the wreckage of the past and make good on our commitment to let God run our lives. In the process, God will show us how to bring others to this spiritually rewarding way of life:

Those who have surrendered and made complete atonement for their wrongs to other people, are in agreement that they have never, whatever the cost has been to them, regretted making restitution. It often requires more courage than some of us can imagine ourselves possessing, but those who wish to put themselves right with God know they must also put themselves right with their fellows.
(*What Is the Oxford Group?*, p. 58, edited)

Making amends is a way of getting out of self and into the Divine. It is amazing that, invariably, God puts someone on our amends list who is in trouble and needs our help. We just don't know who this person is ahead of time. That is why we can not pick and choose which amends to make. If we have prayed about it, discussed the situation with our sharing partner, and received guidance to proceed, we must step out in faith to do the next right thing.

When we right the wrongs, God provides us with the opportunity to "change the world–one life at a time." The first life to be transformed is our own. In addition, we have been given the spiritual tools to alter the lives of others and, in the process, grow in the "fellowship of the Spirit."

10
Step 4: Guidance

Once we have made our surrender, completed our inventories and started on our amends, we are ready to focus our attention on two-way prayer. This is a daily activity we will practice for the rest of our lives. By taking the time to listen to God, we will receive the health, happiness and peace of mind that comes from knowing God's plan for our lives.

Now that we realize God is guiding us each step of the way, there is no reason to ever return to the darkness of anger, fear, shame and guilt. Knowing God wants only the best for us, God will provide everything we need as long as we "perform His work well."

"Fear of economic insecurity will leave us." "When God guides, God provides" becomes our new way of looking at the world and its material instability. It is as simple as that. God will take care of our every need if we are in direct contact with our Creator and follow Divine Guidance.

Anyone who regularly practices two-way prayer is a changed person. This is the essence of a spiritual awakening–listening to the voice of God instead of the voice of self.

We will complete our spiritual journey through the Steps by examining the *How to Listen to God* pamphlet in detail and comparing the words of John Batterson to those of other Group authors. But, before we do this we need to emphasize the importance of two-way prayer.

In 1936, C. Irving Benson wrote a book titled *The Eight Points of the Oxford Group*. This book contains a statement about the current state of the world's affairs that is just as relevant today as when it was written:

> If ever a generation needed to learn stillness, it is ours. We live as though our lives were intended to exemplify the theory of perpetual motion. We live in an intense, over-driven, nervous age, hurried and bustling, noisy and restless. Rush is taking a terrible toll on our lives. As a result, we are suffering from new diseases, not only of the body but of the spirit.
> (*The Eight Points of the Oxford Group*, p. 59, edited)

We are being physically, mentally and spiritually destroyed by our pursuit of "false gods." Our persistent striving for fortune and fame leaves us with a hole in our soul which only God can fill:

> Like gamblers around a roulette table, we are all too absorbed in this game of life. At breakneck speed we rush about altogether too busy to think of the consequences. Nevertheless, we are emerging as a race of nervous wrecks living without harmony or cooperation.
> (*The Eight Points of the Oxford Group*, p. 59, edited)

We burn energy foolishly when we rush aimlessly about fueling the fires of self-will. If nervous energy is the problem, getting quiet is part of the solution:

> Stillness is a real cure for the fatigue to which the inhabitants of this machine age are always liable. Overstrain is as much a cause of moral ruin as is alcohol. When we acquire the art of being still, we recover that peace and serenity which brings our whole being into harmony with God's universe. We restore the rhythm in the billions of cells which compose the brain and body. The remedy for a neurotic age is so simple. We can apply it anyplace at anytime if we are willing to become as little children and learn.
> (*The Eight Points of the Oxford Group*, p. 60, edited)

The key to establishing and maintaining a direct line of communication with God is the "quiet time." It is a discipline anyone can master—a process that provides a positive solution to all the problems of the mind, body and spirit:

> *Guidance* and the *Quiet Time*. A concept equal in importance to the "changed life" is that of Guidance. So far as the Group has any central teaching it is that God will give guidance to those who listen for it with the sincere intent to put it into practice. Neither Buchman nor the Group will maintain that they originated the concept, but every member will emphasize its importance. "Everyone can listen to God." "The only sane people in an insane world are those guided by God." "Definite direction and accurate information can still come from the Mind of God to the mind of man.
> (*The Oxford Group-Its History and Significance*, p. 29, edited)

The author of *What Is the Oxford Group?* confirms that listening to God is a skill worth developing:

> The Group realizes that guidance is not anyone's particular property; it is as free to all of us as are the sun and air, and that there is no reason why everyone, whatever their status or creed, cannot come out of the darkness to breathe the clear and spiritual health-giving properties of God's radiant counsel.
> (*What Is the Oxford Group?*, p. 67, edited)

Guidance will help us face and walk through our fears. What may seem at first to be an impossible situation becomes an opportunity to demonstrate the strength and power of God in our lives:

> Divine guidance takes away from us that fear of tomorrow which, in conjunction with the troubles of today, so often makes life intolerable for us. Not only is today in God's keeping but so is tomorrow. We have surrendered that to God also. Fear of the future, whether it be tomorrow or old age, means that we do not trust in God's guidance.
> (*What Is the Oxford Group?*, p. 67, edited)

For some of us, this is a difficult concept to accept but it is true nevertheless–we live in fear because we do not trust God. Listening to, trusting and following God's guidance are the guiding principles of most religions:

> "Be still and know that I am God." There is a reciprocity between the two statements in this sentence. To know God we must be still. To be still we must know God.

There must be silence in order to know God. The hurried mind and the distracted heart make a vital knowledge of God impossible. When we are ruffled, troubled about many things, in a state of agitation and flutter, we are not conscious of God. As a result, there can be no receptive quietness.
(*The Eight Points of the Oxford Group*, p. 63, edited)

We need to learn how to get quiet so we can discover God's plan for our lives. It is time to "Let go and let God":

God has a plan for every life. He will make known to us His plan day by day if we give Him a chance. But how can God teach us if we have no time to sit in the school of stillness? God can scarcely work an idea in edgeways into our preoccupied minds.

Be still—Leave off—Let be. "Desist from your own attempts and know that I am God." God cannot do very much for us so long as we insist on playing the part of Providence ourselves. Things begin to happen when we "let go and let God." He is God—not you.
(*The Eight Points of the Oxford Group*, pp. 65, 68)

The most productive time to practice two-way prayer is upon awakening. During the brief period before the "committee" convenes and tries to take control of our mind, we have the opportunity to make contact and listen to the source of all that is positive and good in the world.

We make contact by inviting God to join us during our "quiet time" and asking the Divine Inner Voice to direct our thoughts throughout the day.

A "Quiet Time" with the Holy Spirit every morning before "the daily toil and common round" of the world commences will put us in the right key for the day. These early morning "Quiet Times" in which God impresses on our minds His counsel become living spots in the routine of ordinary life.
(*What is the Oxford Group?*, p. 68)

And morning is emphatically the best time. The opening of the day with quiet thought, planning and prayer, is so obviously the right start. This has been the universal experience of the men and women who have lived nearest God throughout the centuries.
(*When Man Listens*, p. 36, edited)

Our mind needs to be free of worry and indecision in order for our "quiet time" to be effective and productive:

It is necessary in our "Quiet Time" to give our mind to God free from doubts and distractions. We must be convinced that God can, and will, tell us what is best for us to do, or not to do, in the plan of our daily lives, or in any problem which confronts us.
(*What Is the Oxford Group?*, p. 70, edited)

It is important we realize we do not have to clear our mind of all thoughts before we can hear the voice of God. Rather, we monitor our thoughts so we can separate the Divine Voice from the self-voice. Emptying the mind is an example of self trying to control self. Usually this effort leaves us frustrated, disillusioned, and even further removed from God's strength and direction:

This does not mean that, when we have a "quiet time," we resign our reasoning powers. The idea that

listening to God means making your mind a blank is a curious misconception which has hindered many people. It does mean that you leave room for God to lead you beyond your human thoughts, and tell you things you could never know yourself.
(*When Man Listens*, p. 34, edited)

This is a revelation, especially to those of us who have spent much of our lives trying to become one with the universe by emptying the mind. Since God speaks to us through our thoughts, we cut ourselves off from God when we try to control, direct or eliminate our thoughts.

We become in tune with the Infinite by listening and following God's guidance, rather than repeating endless mantras. We have found this ritual to be of little value in our attempt to learn God's plan for our lives:

If we truly believe in Guidance, we must recognize that it is not necessary to ask God numberless times for help in a difficult situation. St. Matthew said, "Use not vain repetitions."
(*What is the Oxford Group?*, p. 70)

Listening to God produces results. A. J. Russell describes how he felt the presence of God during his "quiet time":

During "Quiet Times" I have a sense of God being in my head, whereas previously I thought only my own unconsecrated thoughts. Now I find myself asking Him to direct my thinking.
(*For Sinners Only*, p. 307, edited)

"Quiet time" is a two-step process. First we invite God into our lives and then we listen to what God has to say. So two-way prayer consists of a petition followed by quiet listening. It is as simple as that:

> Prayer is the natural complement of God Direction. We cannot expect God to talk to us if we do not talk to Him. It is not always necessary to continually ask God for help in every move we make, or in every problem of our daily lives. If we have faithfully surrendered our lives, God is our Pilot and knows our every movement and thought. When we listen for Guidance during our "Quiet Times" all requests asked or unasked are answered.
> (*What is the Oxford Group?*, p. 69, edited)

The key to the success of two-way prayer is in the listening. We must be willing to hear everything God has to say. Selective hearing does not work any more than does selective honesty or selective restitution:

> There is one condition to be fulfilled before we begin. We must be willing to hear anything God says to us. It is useless to seek God's guidance in one area of life when we are not prepared for God to talk to us about certain other areas. If we want guidance about our family, we may have to listen to some things God has to tell us about ourselves, our character and habits. If it is personal problems, worries or health for which we need direction, we may have to face what God has to say about the way we run our business, or about our attitude toward money. It is all or nothing. Before you begin to listen to God, you must get rid of any known reservations.
> (*When Man Listens*, p. 31, edited)

The *How to Listen to God* pamphlet opens with a challenge

which is to try two-way prayer. As those of us who are using this pamphlet will attest, two-way prayer is the most important discipline we can ever learn:

> **These are a few simple suggestions for people who are willing to make an experiment. You can discover for yourself the most important and practical thing any human being can ever learn — how to be in touch with God.**
>
> **All that is needed is the *willingness to try it honestly*. Every person who has done this consistently and sincerely has found that it really works.**

Then the author provides a brief summary of the assumptions upon which the process of two-way prayer is based. The sheer simplicity of two-way prayer is truly amazing. It is because of this simplicity that anyone, who is willing, can discover how to listen to the Divine Inner Voice:

> **Before you begin, look over these fundamental points. They are true and are based on the experience of thousands of people.**
>
> **1. God is alive. He always has been and He always will be.**
>
> **2. God knows everything.**
>
> **3. God can do anything.**
>
> **4. God can be everywhere--all at the same time. (These are the important differences between God and us human beings.)**

5. God is invisible–we can't see Him or touch Him–but <u>*God is here*</u>. He is with you now. He is beside you. He surrounds you. He fills the room or the whole place where you are right now. <u>*He is in you now*</u>. <u>*He is in your heart*</u>.

6. God cares very much for <u>*you*</u>. He is interested in you. He has a plan for your life. He has an answer for every need and problem you face.

7. God will tell you all that you <u>*need*</u> to know. He will not always tell you all that you <u>*want*</u> to know.

8. God will help you do anything that He asks you to do.

The author then provides an overview of the steps which, if followed, will result in direct, two-way communion with the Divine Spirit within. This process puts us directly in contact with God:

9. Anyone can be in touch with God, anywhere and at any time, <u>*if the conditions are obeyed*</u>.

These are the conditions:

- To be quiet and still,
- To listen,
- To be honest about every thought that comes,
- To test the thoughts to be sure that they come from God, and
- To obey.

The author writes detailed descriptions for each step, so

there can be no question or confusion as to what needs to be done. First we must make the necessary preparations so we can hear what God has to say:

> **So, with these basic elements as a background, here are specific suggestions on _How to Listen to God:_**
>
> **1. *Take Time***
> **Find some place and time where you can be alone, quiet and undisturbed. Most people have found that the early morning is the best time. Have with you some paper and pen or pencil.**
>
> **2. *Relax***
> **Sit in a comfortable position. Consciously relax all your muscles. Be loose. There is no hurry. There needs to be no strain during these minutes. God cannot get through to us if we are tense and anxious about later responsibilities.**
>
> **3. *Tune In***
> **Open your heart to God. Either silently or aloud, just say to God in a natural way that you would like to find His plan for your life—you want His answer to the problem or situation that you are facing just now. Be definite and specific in your request.**

We must realize that listening to God does take effort and time. It is a process that cannot be hurried or held to specific time limits. This is like telling God that our time is more valuable than His. A. J. Russell explains the need to set aside whatever time it takes to make contact:

> Listening to God takes time. It takes a lot more time than the brief address to God which we call

"saying our prayers." It takes time because God has to get through so many layers of our human, self-governed, self-centered thinking before God can communicate with us. It takes time because God leads us in "quiet time" into the thorough constructive planning of our life in partnership with Him.

It is true that God intends for us to live in such a manner that we are constantly in contact with Him. In this way, God can speak to us at any time. But the men and women who have known God best have invariably found that they could not maintain constant contact without daily time spent quietly alone with the Holy Spirit.
(*When Man Listens,* p. 36, edited)

We are being foolish when we say we have no time to listen. What could possibly be more important than determining God's plan for us each and every day?

It is possible to challenge those who cannot seem to find time to practice two-way prayer with this thought provoking question: "What? No time for God?" How selfish we are when we put ourselves first and try to live without the care and protection of the One who created us in the first place:

Most of us, when we say we have no time, are simply dishonest. Some of us have not realized how much time later in the day is saved through added efficiency, through clearer selection of what is important and what should be left, through the greater strength and peace which come when we have listened to God and received specific directions for our day.

(*When Man Listens*, p. 36, edited)

Eleanore Napier-Forde tells us that by listening to the Voice of God we can overcome the voice of self and prevent anxiety and confusion from ruining our lives. When we are overwhelmed with busyness, it is impossible for God to get through:

> The Quiet Time is so important because it is only there that we can shut out the world with its clamor of duty, its conflicting appeals, and our own tangled thoughts, and realize the presence of God.

> We need enough time to forget time, and this often means the sacrifice of other interests and almost inevitably that last precious hour of morning sleep. It is not too much to say that for many people the power of the whole day completely depends on that first hour alone with God. The man who would move mountains must give God his ear before the rush of life is upon him. For many it may involve the discipline of getting up earlier and letting God organize your day so that everything in God's plan for that day will be done.
> (*The Guidance of God*, pp. 23-24, edited)

Take time–do not hurry. This is valuable advice if we are to overcome our addiction to noise and activity:

> It is absolutely necessary that this "Quiet Time" be leisurely and unhurried. Haste is the death of two-way prayer.

> At first you may be bored. You will want to do something or talk to someone. You are probably an activity junkie, a noise drunkard. But keep on.

(The Eight Points of the Oxford Group, p. 71, edited)

Now that we have made the necessary preparations, it is time to listen:

4. *Listen*
Just be still, quiet, relaxed and open. Let your mind go "loose." Let God do the talking. Thoughts, ideas, and impressions will begin to come into your mind and heart. Be alert and aware and open to every one.

God speaks to us through our mind using our own words. This is why God has been described as "a still small voice." It is reassuring to know that the voice we hear is our own. This reduces any fear we may have about listening.

Next, the author instructs us to capture our thoughts by writing them down. This is the most important part of the entire process–putting on paper what we hear. Do not question the thoughts; just record them for later review.

Many of us record our thoughts in guidance books. We do this for four reasons: first, so we will not forget what we have heard during our time alone with God; second, so we can test our guidance to separate the self-thoughts from the God thoughts; third, so we can discuss our guidance with our sharing partners; and fourth, so we can critique our activities to see if we have, in fact, followed God's plan for us that day.

For those who are skeptical about the need to write, ask yourselves, "How can I determine if I have followed God's guidance for the day, if I cannot even remember what it was God wanted me to?" Many of us find that, if not recorded, the thoughts we receive during our "quiet time" are quickly forgotten:

5. *Write!*
Here is the important key to the whole process.
Write down everything that comes into your mind.
Everything. Writing is simply a means of recording
so that you can remember later. *Don't* sort out or
edit your thoughts at this point.

Don't say to yourself:
> This thought isn't important;
> This is just an ordinary thought;
> This can't be guidance;
> This isn't nice;
> This can't be from God;
> This is just me thinking, etc.

Write down everything that passes through your mind:
> Names of people;
> Things to do;
> Things to say;
> Things that are wrong and need to be made
> right.

Write down everything:
> Good thoughts–bad thoughts;
> Comfortable thoughts–uncomfortable thoughts;
> "Holy" thoughts–"unholy" thoughts;
> Sensible thoughts–"crazy" thoughts.

Be Honest! Write down *everything*. A thought
comes quickly, and it escapes even more quickly
unless it is captured and put down.

We record our thoughts because it is important to have

written evidence of God's plan for our lives:

> The Group advocates our use of a pencil and notebook so that we may record every God given thought and idea that comes to us during our time alone with Him, that no detail, however small, may be lost to us and that we may not shirk the truth about ourselves or any problem, when it comes to us.
> (*What Is the Oxford Group?*, p. 68)

> The Group strongly recommends the keeping of a Guidance Book wherein we write the inspired thoughts that come in waiting. I used to smile at this as a very kindergarten method. But I can now testify that it is abundantly worthwhile. I had no idea how well it worked until I tried it. Suggestions are soon crowded out in the day's business unless we make a note of them at once. If inspirations are not captured and acted upon, they soon evaporate.
> (*The Eight Points of the Oxford Group*, p. 70, edited)

As described in a previous chapter, James Houck has provided us with an alternative to written guidance for those who have difficulty writing or cannot write fast enough to keep up with their thoughts. This is the concept of "fingertip guidance."

With this technique we touch our thumb to a finger to capture a thought. It can be very effective when we are not in a position to write, such as when driving a car or taking a shower. Up to eight thoughts can be captured this way. These thoughts can later be relayed to a sharing partner or to fellow team members during a Guidance meeting.

Many of us who write guidance use "fingertip guidance"

from time to time. We wait until the end of our "quiet time" to record the thoughts we have captured. This procedure significantly reduces the amount of paper used to record thoughts and provides the equivalent of an "executive summary" for the session.

After we write down or capture our thoughts, we need to test what we have written to separate the God thoughts from the self-thoughts. Here is where the Four Standards of Honesty, Purity, Unselfishness and Love are so important.

This is how it works. After the thoughts have slowed or we have stopped writing, we look over what we have put on paper. There is a good chance the thoughts which pass the test of Honesty, Purity, Unselfishness and Love are from God; conversely those thoughts which are dishonest, impure, selfish and fearful are based in self.

We test our thoughts because not all of them come from God. There are two voices trying to get our attention, and we must be able to tell the difference between them. Some describe these as the Voice of God and the voice of self:

6. *Test*
When the flow of thoughts slows down, stop. Take a good look at what you have written. _Not every thought we have comes from God._ So we need to test our thoughts. Here is where the written record helps us to be able to look at them.

a) Are these thoughts completely _honest, pure, unselfish and loving?_
b) Are these thoughts in line with our duties to our family–to our country?
c) Are these thoughts in line with our under-

standing of the teachings found in our spiritual literature?

The author of *What Is the Oxford Group?* provides us with some very practical reasons for testing our guidance:

> It is not suggested that everything we write down during our Quiet Times necessarily comes from God. The human mind, being what it is, wanders from concentration at an outside interruption, takes up a train of thought it finds hard to discard, invents or remembers a thought of its own. But to those closely in touch with God it becomes easy after a short while to differentiate between spiritual and human messages.
> (*What Is the Oxford Group?*, p. 68)

By testing guidance, we learn where we need to make additional surrenders, conduct additional inventories, and carry out additional restitutions. Taking the Steps is an ongoing process that brings us closer and closer to God each time we take the actions necessary to "(perform) His work well."

Eleanor Forde-Napier also tells us to test our thoughts. If we skip this vital procedure, we can end up with journal after journal containing streams of consciousness which may or may not have anything to do with guidance from God:

> Guidance, left to itself, has no anchor. Since the most important thing about Guidance is the one from whom it comes, we must be sure we know the source of what we put on paper. As we reach out into the realm of the spirit, we can hear the aged Apostle warning us: "Believe not every spirit, but test the spirits (to determine) whether they are of God." (1

John 4:1)
(*The Guidance of God*, p. 4, edited)

As part of the test, we need to determine what another person who is practicing two-way prayer thinks of our guidance. We may believe our thoughts are from God, but, since we have a difficult time seeing ourselves as we really are, it is important that we check our guidance with a sharing partner:

7.   Check
When in doubt and when it is important, what does another person who is living two-way prayer think about this thought or action? More light comes in through two windows than one. Someone else who also wants God's plan for our lives may help us to see more clearly.

Talk over together what you have written. Many people do this. They tell each other what guidance has come. This is the secret of unity. There are always three sides to every question—your side, my side, and the right side. Guidance shows us which is the right side—not who is right, but what is right.

"More light comes in through two windows than one." God speaks to us through others as well as through our thoughts. This reliance upon a sharing partner is essential if we are to receive full benefit from our times alone with God. We need to check our guidance to protect ourselves from "all sorts of absurd actions and ideas":

An observer who listens to the process of sharing guidance, which usually follows the "quiet time," will be struck by the fact that much of the guidance will be

of a very obvious and commonplace character. Even so, the observer must keep in mind that not everything that appears to be guidance comes from God. To guard against unwise action–for many foolish things have been done which were purported to be the will of God — the Group has developed the practice of "checking" guidance. This is the submission of guidance to the judgment of one or more Group members for advice. Also no guidance is looked on as genuine which violates the Four Standards.
(*The Oxford Group-Its History and Significance*, p. 30, edited)

Many Group members attend weekly Guidance meetings. We share what we have received during our "quiet times" at these gatherings for two reasons. First, it shows those who are still skeptical or are having difficulty with two-way prayer that the process really works. Second, on many occasions the guidance we receive is not for us but for someone else in the room.

Sharing guidance at weekly meetings provides us the opportunity to expand our awareness of God's plan for our lives and to grow in the "Fellowship of the Spirit." It also demonstrates the power of Group guidance:

"What say others to whom God speaks?" This is the unwritten law of fellowship. There is no place for the temperamental whims of a person who likes to play the rogue elephant-the person who resents the constraining discipline of the team-whose loyalty has no wider scope than his vanity. Fellowship requires that each of us must be ready to let any plan of our own, however good, be superseded if God reveals a

better one through other people.
(*The Guidance of God*, pp. 21-22, edited)

Next, we address what for some of us is the hardest part of all, which is to obey the guidance we receive. In order to successfully follow through on guidance, we must step out in faith and trust God to direct our every thought and deed:

8. *Obey*
Carry out the thoughts that have come. You will only be sure of guidance as you go through with it. A rudder will not guide a boat until the boat is moving. As you obey, very often the results will convince you that you are on the right track.

We have to move beyond just thinking and talking about guidance. We must take action. Sometimes this requires the sacrifice of time, energy and money. But, when we look back upon our efforts to implement guidance, we realize God's plan was far better than anything we could have come up with on our own. God has definitely done for us what we could not do for ourselves.

It is a relief to know that God will never provide us with a plan without the strength or financial resources to implement it:

When a God thought comes into our minds, we sometimes doubt its authenticity. We say to ourselves, "It's all very well to get guidance, but what use is it without the practical means to carry it out?" When we think these thoughts, we are forgetting that God never guides us to do anything He does not give us the means to make happen. Faith is the assurance of things hoped for, the proving of things

not seen. If we trust and go right ahead to carry out God's instructions, however obscure the means or the objective may seem to us, it is amazing to the unenlightened minds how God not only provides the guidance but the assistance and the outcome which is best for us according to His Plan.
(*What Is the Oxford Group?*, p. 71, edited)

Obeying Guidance requires faith. If we take care of our part, which is to implement our God thoughts, and let God take care of the outcome, we are amazed at how much easier life becomes. When we maintain an open channel to God, we are able to accomplish what, at one time, seemed entirely out of reach:

> We must be prepared to let God manage all our affairs. God will direct our time, money, relationships—in fact, everything we possess. It might mean giving your time in a Sunday School or helping your neighbor if he or she is too ill or too poor to pay for help. It might mean modifying your attitude towards clothes or food or drink. It might mean surrendering to God the royalties of a play or book, as Hugh Redwood did with his fine story *God in the Slums*.
> (*For Sinners Only*, p. 41, edited)

It is important to remember that God has given us free will—we are free *not* to listen to God's guidance. But, we must be prepared to accept the consequences if we choose not to follow our Creator's plan for our lives.

But, what if we do not hear any definite messages when we listen to God. Let us assure you, this can happen at any time. It means that we have additional work to do. We need to revisit one or more of the Steps so we can get reconnected:

9. Blocks?

What if I don't seem to get any definite thoughts? God's guidance is as freely available as the air we breathe. If I am not receiving thoughts when I listen the fault is not God's.

Usually it is because there is something _I will not do_:
something wrong in my life that I will not face and make right;
a habit or indulgence I will not give up;
a person I will not forgive;
a wrong relationship in my life I will not give up;
a restitution I will not make;
something God has already told me to do that I will not obey.

Check these points and be honest. Then try listening again.

If we do not hear any definite thoughts during our meditation, it is a sign we have not completely cleaned up the wreckage of the past. We need to review our assets and liabilities checklist to determine if we have additional work to do and check our amends list to make sure we have completed all restitutions. If we are unwilling to proceed with an amends, there is a good chance we will remain separated from the "One who has all power."

What if we follow guidance and realize somewhere along the line we have made a mistake? The voice we thought was God's turns out to be self-will after all. We are human and we do make mistakes:

10. Mistakes

Suppose I make a mistake and do something in the name of God that isn't right? Of course we make mistakes. We are humans with many faults. However, *God will always honor our sincerity.*

He will work around and through every honest mistake we make. He will help us make it right. *But remember this!* sometimes when we do obey God, someone else may not like it or agree with it. So when there is opposition, it doesn't always mean you have made a mistake. It can mean that the other person doesn't want to know or to do what is right.

Suppose I fail to do something that I have been told and the opportunity to do it passes? There is only one thing to do. Put it right with God. Tell Him you're sorry. Ask Him to forgive you, then accept His forgiveness and begin again. God is our Father—He is not an impersonal calculator. He understand us far better than we do.

Sometimes we will not have the blessings of those around us as we carry out God's plan for our lives. Everyone is not listening to God. Some people find us a threat to their selfish, self-centered lifestyles. They would rather retaliate against us than look at themselves. Others are just suspicious or misinformed about our intentions. But, we must continue to demonstrate the power of two-way prayer by letting God's love radiate through us:

The guided life is a blessed life. By listening to God, more and more of our thoughts and actions are freed from the bondage of hate, fear, indulgence, prejudice and ignorance. We are now at liberty to

follow God's will. *Guidance does work.* That is our final confirmation.
(*When Man Listens*, p. 36, edited)

Yes miracles occur when we are willing to follow God's directions. We find a new peace and a new happiness beyond our wildest dreams when we practice two-way prayer. Our lives have changed–we are reborn:

11. *Results*
We never know what swimming is like until we get down into the water and try. We will never know what this is like until we sincerely try it.

Every person who has tried this honestly finds that a wisdom, not their own, comes into their minds and that Power greater than human power begins to operate in their lives. It is an endless adventure.

There is a way of life, for everyone, everywhere. Anyone can be in touch with the living God, anywhere, anytime, *if we fulfill His Conditions*:

> **When man listens, God Speaks.**
> **When man obeys, God Acts.**

This is the law of prayer.

God's plan for this world goes forward through the lives of ordinary people who are willing to be governed by Him.

In *I Was a Pagan*, Victor Kitchen explains how listening to God has changed his life and the lives of those around him. In

previous chapters of this book, Victor has shown us how he
took the Steps of Surrender, Sharing and Restitution. He is now
ready to practice two-way prayer and become a life-changer.

This section of *I Was a Pagan* opens with Victor talking to a
member of the Group. Victor has never practiced two-way
prayer, and his new found friend is taking him through the
process:

> Victor, you have told me you believe God has
> some kind of a plan and method for developing the
> personality or soul of human beings. You believe it is
> everyone's duty to cooperate with that plan. Rather
> than being in conflict with or in opposition to what is
> actually going on in the universe, you believe people
> should consciously enter into the scheme of things
> and deliberately *try* to grow a soul. And yet you say
> you don't know how to do it. You don't know how to
> apply your beliefs. You don't know how to get in
> touch with God.
> (*I Was a Pagan*, p. 55, edited)

The Group member describes the basics of two-way prayer,
but Victor is skeptical. Afterwards, Victor reviews what the
man has just told him:

> The idea of getting directly in touch with God–
> asking Him questions and getting answers and
> directions on how to conduct my life–seemed to me
> an out-and-out absurdity. Yet he said it could be
> done. He said he was doing it himself and that was
> what gave him the power to *apply* beliefs and *carry out*
> the plan of God–power that I did not have. He said I
> could have it, just as he did, if I would pay the same
> price, comply with the same conditions, and go

through the same series of exceedingly simple Steps.
(*I Was a Pagan*, p. 56, edited)

The Steps the Group member is referring to are Surrender, Sharing, Restitution and Guidance. He explains that Victor has made a Surrender, but he has additional work to do. Victor takes the remaining three Steps and experiences a spiritual transformation. This is one of the greatest rewards of the program, a new way of living without obsessions, compulsions, or self-centered behaviors. Victor describes his spiritual experience as the opening of a two-way channel to God:

> At that moment, I became distinctly conscious of a force flowing through me. At first, while I was praying for the things I wanted, this force seemed to gather within me and flowed upward and outward as though I were broadcasting my wish to God and asking Him to do something about it. However, the moment I asked God to take over, the flow definitely stopped. Then, it started in the opposite direction. It was as though an idea generated outside of me had been broadcast from space, entering my mind and flowing downward to become the wish of my being. I was not only changed, but completely turned around.
> (*I Was a Pagan*, p. 83, edited)

Yes, Victor has changed. He is not the same person he was before he heard the voice of God–a simple voice that spoke to him through his thoughts. Victor immediately realizes he needs God's guidance in every area of his life:

> Prior to this experience, I realized that my prayers had been little but wishful thinking–that I had prayed to God chiefly to bring about the things I wanted, in

the way I wanted them to come. I then and there
asked God to take over my prayer and guide it, so
that I might pray for what He wanted me to bring
about–so that He might use me for His purpose
instead of my trying to use Him for mine.
(*I Was a Pagan*, p. 82, edited)

Victor describes how God is now guiding him in his
daily affairs and through all of his difficulties:

God today is teaching me directly through my
daily "quiet time" in the morning and indirectly
through the books He guides me to read, through the
Group meetings He guides me to attend, through the
rich experiences He leads me into, and through the
difficulties He uses to develop my moral fiber. In this
instruction, He brings me down to the very essentials
of living. He wastes no words in superficialities. He
tells me what I am living for and there is no mistaking
what His plan is for me.
(*I Was a Pagan*, p. 98, edited)

Victor and his wife become sharing partners. Sharing
guidance helps strengthen their marriage by minimizing
conflict and misunderstandings:

My wife and I began to pray together for a new
vision of the couple God would have us be. One of
our greatest blessings, as my wife says now, is finding
ourselves telling one another our own weak spots and
asking for one another's prayers about them, with no
fear that the other will gloat about it or use that
confidence as a weapon in the future. Instead, of
criticizing each other, we now criticize ourselves to
each other, and ask the other's prayers about it.

Guided living eliminates the frictions which are bound to arise when two self-centered people are brought into close proximity. There is little friction between my wife and myself now because, when we have a difference of opinion, we have a "quiet time" and refer the matter to God.
(*I Was a Pagan*, pp. 111-112, edited)

Victor receives guidance which helps his financial situation. In addition, God provides Victor with additional time to spend helping others:

At another time, now just about a year ago, God guided me to make a certain investment in an enterprise I have never before known about, and which I would not even have considered on a human basis. God promised me that this investment would give me more time and opportunity to do His work. It has been that very investment which has provided me with the time to write a book, take certain trips with the Group, and engage in other phases of creative spiritual activity.
(*I Was a Pagan*, pp. 121-122, edited)

Victor is happier than he has ever been and much more attuned to living life on life's terms. His enthusiasm and positive attitude are infectious. For the first time, Victor realizes his primary purpose is to fit himself "to be of maximum service to God and the people about (him)":

I was no longer vexed, distressed, or worried when people spoke against me. I remained calm and happy regardless of circumstances. I started appreciating the beauty in nature and the infinite goodness of God. I found a future, stretching through eternity

and which, for the first time, held a sure salvation for myself, for my family and for those who would reach out a seeking hand. To live out of touch with God is to miss the whole point of life.
(*I Was a Pagan*, pp. 178, 182-183, edited)

To live a life of service to God and mankind must seem irrational to those who have yet to experience the presence of God. But, when we rely upon God, "common sense (will) thus become uncommon sense." Great events will come to pass for anyone who is willing to listen to God. This is a guarantee:

> What can we expect as we grow more experienced in this listening to God? Probably the first thing we realize will be that the whole level of our thinking has been altered. We shall see that what we took for sound reasoning before was just our human thinking, dictated by self-will, prejudice, fear, or limited by the fact that we were leaving God out of the picture. The judgment of a surrendered person who listens to God is something beyond human reason.
> (*When Man Listens*, p. 34, edited)

Yes, we offer a new way of living without addictions, afflictions, compulsive behaviors, loneliness or despair. Guidance is being used daily by people from every walk of life. "Quiet times" are being practiced in both living rooms and board rooms, in small gatherings and large assemblies, in our homes and our churches. It works, because no matter what the problem, God is the solution–no matter what the question, two-way prayer is the answer.

11

The Five C's of Life-Changing

The next phase of our spiritual development is to carry our life-changing message to others. We strengthen and expand our conversion experience when we work with those who have yet to witness the miracle of two-way prayer. All around us people are trapped in the living Hell of their addictions, compulsions, fears and avarice because they do not know how to listen to God. We can now be of benefit to them and in the process change their lives:

> The young will find there is a purpose in their future which is not dull and uninteresting, but adventurous and worthwhile. The old will learn that each day of additional life is a day they can live to its fullest, and that all vain regrets for the past are as useless as a storm that has passed over and is gone.
> (*What Is the Oxford Group?*, p. 5, edited)

In *What Is the Oxford Group?*, the author tells us we can all become life-changers if we just practice and implement the technique of two-way prayer:

> The spiritual activities of listening to God and following guidance have proven indispensable to the countless numbers who are living changed lives. They are not new ideas nor inventions of the Group. They are

based on universal spiritual truths.

> We cannot all be great thinkers or talkers for God.
> But, all of us can become life-changers by utilizing those
> God given abilities which are best suited for the
> purpose. In this crisis-filled world, the person whose
> domain is the household is just as important to God as
> the ruler of a nation. To all of us in our different ways
> God issues a challenge for a new world–a world that
> listens to God.
> (*What Is the Oxford Group?*, p. 8, 131, edited)

In 1917, Frank Buchman summarized the process of life-
changing as the Five C's of Confidence, Confession, Conviction,
Conversion and Continuance. In his book titled *Life Changers*,
Harold Begbie describes how Frank developed the concept of the
Five C's during an ocean voyage to the Far East. At dinner, a young
lady asked him how "an ordinary person like herself" could change
others:

> "But," she cautioned, "if you tell me, you must tell
> me very simply." In his "quiet time" the next morning,
> these five words came to him and he wrote them
> down–Confidence, Confession, Conviction, Conversion,
> Continuance.
> (*Life Changers*, p.169)

Once again, we see the importance of writing down our
guidance. If Frank had not put on paper what he heard during his
"quiet time," we would not have this simple, yet very effective
method for taking people to a better way of life.

Walter Clark provides a clear, concise overview of the Five C's
in his book, *The Oxford Group–Its History and Significance*:

Confidence involves the establishment of rapport by
the life-changer with the person to be changed.
Confession involves the admission of faults that the
"changed" individual has overcome for the purpose of
encouraging prospective converts. Conviction is the
mental process by which the "unchanged" becomes
aware of his or her shortcomings. Conversion is the
change itself, which includes a commitment to forsake
sin and follow God's guidance. Not even a prior belief
in God is strictly necessary. To act *as if* there were a
God is sufficient; a genuine belief in God frequently
follows.   Continuance involves the activity which
strengthens and confirms conversion by seeking and
following guidance, and "changing" others.
(*The Oxford Group–Its History and Significance*, p. 28,
edited)

In 1919, Howard Walter wrote *Soul Surgery*. Throughout the
book, he describes the process of life-changing. He compares the
work to that of a doctor. Just as the surgeon heals diseased bodies,
the life-changer heals diseased souls.

The author writes that we will receive the strength and
guidance to successfully change others during our morning "quiet
time":

In the first place, *through early morning prayer* our
own spirits are brought in tune with the infinite. We are
made spiritually sensitive, strong and resourceful in
order to meet all the opportunities that await us in the
days to come. Our intuitive understanding is enhanced,
so we are likely to view things in the right perspective,
looking at certain seeming interruptions that may come
as God-sent opportunities for service, and refusing to
allow the most important work of all to be crowded into

a corner or out of the day altogether. We can all plead
the excuse of busyness, but many of the busiest people
are the greatest life-changers; they have learned to "put
first things first" at all costs.
(*Soul Surgery*, pp. 41-42, edited)

Let us put "first things first" and have Howard Walter guide us
through the Five C's of life-changing. Then, we will use the Oxford
Group pamphlet titled *How Do I Begin?* to apply the Five C's to our
life saving efforts.

1. Confidence

We must use our God given skills in a way that convinces our
prospects that we know what we are talking about. It is essential to
get into the trenches and communicate at a level the prospect
understands:

> The physician of souls must know his patients
> intimately, or he cannot diagnose their troubles
> accurately. If it is worthwhile for the salesman of a
> business to study men in order that he may know how
> best to win them to a desire to purchase his wares, how
> much more important is that study for us who would
> win men to a new life of spiritual health and well being.

> Oliver Wendell Holmes says we must become men
> who know men in the street and at their work; human
> nature in its shirt-sleeves. Through first hand experi-
> ence, we have found plenty of praying rogues and
> swearing saints in the world.
> (*Soul Surgery*, pp. 50, 51, edited)

Henry Drummond tells us we have a special gift that the world
desperately needs:

The amount of spiritual longing in the world at the present moment is absolutely incredible. No one can even faintly appreciate the intense spiritual unrest which seethes everywhere around us. But, the one who has begun by private experiment, by looking into himself and by making observations of the people near him, has witnessed a spectacle sufficient to call for the loudest and most emphatic action.
(*Soul Surgery*, p. 56, edited)

Frank Buchman provides us with an example of what happens when our prospects fail to identify with us. Early in his career, Frank had difficulty winning the confidence of others because they could not relate to him:

Dr. Buchman tells of how in his early preaching days he saw no spiritual results. He could not understand what was the trouble. When he asked Rev. F. B. Meyer, for his advice, Mr. Meyer replied, "Tell your people on Sunday the things they have been telling you during the week." The trouble was they had been telling him nothing. He was not in their confidence. His sermons, instead of being woven of the very stuff of their lives–their temptations and doubts and problems and failures–were intellectual dissertations which largely went over the heads of the people and did not touch or move their hearts.
(*Soul Surgery* p. 51, edited)

We need to learn everything we can about our prospect so we can better understand his or her needs and motivations:

The soul-physician must know the soul, in health and disease, and the universal human heart, which is found to be so surprisingly alike in all lands when its

passions and fears and aspirations are analyzed. In addition, he must also know the particular individual to whom God's Spirit has directed him to help with all the power, seen and unseen, that he can muster to his support. As a preliminary step in gaining his confidence, let him study his patient's likes and dislikes, his habits and associations.
(*Soul Surgery*, p. 53, edited)

We must honestly describe some aspect of our lives if we hope to gain the confidence of the prospect:

It is generally understood that if the message is to strike home to the hearts of his hearers, it must proceed from his own heart. That which comes from the heart reaches the heart, as the French proverb says. If life-changing is "truth through personality," as Beecher defined it, it must come charged with the authoritative power of personal experience. He must abandon self, but also give *himself*, his treasured experiences of the soul, if he is to attain the confidence which must precede true friendship and service.
(*Soul Surgery*, pp. 59-60, edited)

In order for us to successfully relate to others, we must genuinely like people and strive to make them feel comfortable with us. General William Booth of the Salvation Army understood this necessity:

The first vital step in saving outcasts consists of making them feel that some decent human being cares enough about them to take an interest in the question of whether they rise or sink.
(*Soul Surgery*, p. 61, edited)

The life-changer must be friendly, loving and compassionate.

These are all characteristics of a person who listens to God and follows Divine guidance:

> It is evident that true "lovers of their fellow-men" do not possess an abstract "love of the crowd" but a warm, sympathetic, enduring interest in individuals around them, which expresses itself in varied forms. And to such men and women the confidence of others naturally comes.
> (*Soul Surgery*, p. 65)

2. Confession

Once we have secured the confidence of the prospect, we acknowledge some shortcoming from our own experience:

> Confession is an extension of confidence, denoting that the life-changer has gotten through to the innermost recesses of his friend's life, has been privileged to see into the darkened chamber whose door is usually closed and barred, so that he knows his man–his motives and the desires that are the roots of all his actions. Through the avenue of confidence we win a man's friendship. Through confession we may win his soul.
> (*Soul Surgery*, p. 66, edited)

We must get to the root of the problem if we are to cure the soul sickness. The spiritual malady manifests itself in many different forms. In order to be effective, "we had to get down to causes and conditions":

> Every physician knows the importance of getting to the root of the trouble, to avoid the danger of false diagnosis and superficial or harmful treatment, which might produce a fatal result. Is it any less important for the soul-surgeon with a life-destiny at stake to make

certain that he has reached the ultimate seat of the trouble before he seeks to administer the cure? It is well for him to remember that men are living their lives on four levels: spiritual, intellectual, social and physical. The diseased spot, the center of infection that is spreading in all directions, may be in any of the four. It may be that either false pride, dishonesty, selfishness or impurity, emanating from any one of the four levels that is slowly poisoning the entire personality.
(*Soul Surgery*, pp. 67-68, edited)

In this passage, we find a test to determine the source of the spiritual malady. False pride, dishonesty, selfishness and impurity constitute a test for self-will. In addition, they are the opposites of the Four Standards of Honesty, Purity, Unselfishness and Love.

Using the test for God's will or for self-will, we focus on our life-changing work. We must be direct and forthright, but at the same time we must not be overbearing or intimidating:

Misdirected spiritual effort will be fruitless or worse, for, by aiming at random, we not only fail to gain the individual but we may spoil the chance of gaining him at a later date.
(*Soul Surgery*, p. 68, edited)

We need to speak in a manner that our prospect will understand. However, it is totally unnecessary and inappropriate to curse or take the Lord's name in vain in order to get our point across. Rather, we use plain, simple, everyday language to carry our message:

Any feeling of superiority on our part is fatal, especially in view of the fact that any such attitude is always unjustifiable. To go with a confession of

unworthiness is not only consistent, but it tends to disarm criticism. Hence, when approaching the prospect, it is always safest and generally helpful to begin by confessing one's own sense of unworthiness.
(*Soul Surgery*, p. 91, edited)

We confess our shortcomings so the prospect will feel safer about sharing his or her character liabilities:

> *Be ready to confess your own shortcomings honestly and humbly.* Nothing will more surely prevent an appearance of self-righteousness in the spiritual physician than his own confession of where he too fell before the onslaughts of temptation, and found, in the power and presence of God, salvation and security.

> God often uses our temptations, and perhaps our early failures and our ultimate victories, to make and keep us modest and sincere in these delicate spiritual operations that need to be performed.
> (*Soul Surgery*, pp. 88-89, edited)

The life-changer must assure the prospect that everything shared between them will be kept in the strictest of confidence. Without this pledge of confidentiality, the prospect will be reluctant or even unwilling to disclose those thoughts and actions which have kept him or her from developing a personal relationship with God:

> Keep every confession absolutely sacred. The necessity for observing this principle may seem obvious. Yet we often do not realize how easy it is to let slip a remark about some person into whose confidence we have come.

> The professional honor of the physician is of the

utmost importance here, as every priest is compelled to
learn. Unless people come to feel an entire reliance on
our discretionary silence they assuredly will not trust us.
Many a potential life-changer has been severely hindered
because he or she never acquired this precious gift of
silence.
(*Soul Surgery*, p. 93, edited)

3. Conviction

Once we have confessed, there is a good chance the prospect will
feel the need to confess also. When the prospect gets honest with the
life-changer, he or she will be convinced of the need for change. In
order for this to occur, the prospect must come to believe that self-will
is the problem and God is the solution. Also, the prospect needs the
conviction to do something about the difficulties which have just
come to light:

Conviction is as closely related to Confession as
Confession is to Confidence. But, confession of difficulties
does not necessarily bring with it the conviction to do
something about them.
(*Soul Surgery*, p. 96, edited)

James Houck describes the process of Conviction in terms of
"hate, forsake, confess and restore." We must first hate the thought or
action which is blocking us off from God before we can overcome its
destructiveness. These blocks manifest themselves in many different
ways, such as fear, resentment, physical or emotional abuse,
alcoholism and drug addiction among others. For example, a drug
addict must reach a point of hating what the drug is doing to the
mind, body and soul before there can be a surrender. If the addict
does not hate the drug, the addict will never forsake the drug. Once
he or she has confessed the addiction, inventoried the damage, made
restitution for the harm and restored two-way communication with

God, there is a good chance of permanent recovery.

Conviction is contagious. In order for the prospect to become convinced, we must ourselves be convinced that God is the answer to all of our problems:

> Character is caught not taught. Before you can get God into anyone else, you must have a contagious case of God yourself. Health is contagious as well as disease. In our presence, the prospect should feel the elation of our radiant, victorious life.

> Interest stimulates interest. Enthusiasm awakens enthusiasm. So it is that a man who has had a genuine spiritual experience is certain to inspire in others, wherever he goes, an interest in spiritual matters and a desire to possess the same power and enthusiasm.
> (*Soul Surgery*, pp. 108, 111, edited)

4. Conversion

Conversion produces psychic change. The prospect's life is transformed from being dominated by self-will to being guided by God's will.

William James provides us with a description of this change in *Varieties of Religious Experience*:

> To be converted, to be regenerated, to receive grace, to gain confidence, are some of the phrases which denote the process, gradual or sudden, by which a person, once separated and spiritless, becomes unified and spirit filled, as a consequence of his or her firm hold upon certain spiritual truths.
> (*Soul Surgery*, p. 119, edited)

In the *Meaning of Faith*, Dr. Harry Emerson Fosdick also describes this spiritual transformation. In this passage, Fosdick tells us where we find God–right inside each and every one of us:

> Conversion begins when the God outwardly argued is inwardly experienced. This transformation begins when we cease to seek Him among the clouds, and retreat into the fertile places of our own spirits. God outside of us is a theory; God inside of us becomes a fact. God outside of us is speculation; God inside of us is an experience.
> (*Soul Surgery*, p. 122, edited)

Testimonials validate the Conversion experience. William James provides us with an example of how a drunkard by the name of S. H. Hadley overcame his difficulties:

> When the invitation was given, I knelt down with a crowd of drunkards. Oh, what a conflict there was going on in my poor soul! A blessed whisper said, "Come." The devil said, "Be careful." I halted but a moment, and then, with a breaking heart, I said, "Dear Jesus, can you help me?" Never with mortal tongue can I describe that moment. Although up to that point my soul had been filled with indescribable gloom, I felt the glorious brightness of the noonday sun shine into my heart. I felt I was a free man. Oh, the precious feeling of safety, of freedom. God with all His brightness and power had come into my life; that indeed, old things had passed away and all things had become new.

> From that moment till now I have never wanted a drink of whiskey, and I have never seen money enough to make me take one. I promised God that night that if He would take away my appetite for strong drink, I

would work for Him all my life. He has done His part,
and I have been trying to do mine.
(*Soul Surgery*, p. 122, edited)

In this short story, William James describes two voices–the Voice
of God and the voice of self. These voices are in conflict with one
another for control of our lives. The voice of God is honest, pure,
unselfish and loving. The voice of self is dishonest, impure, selfish
and fearful. The choice is ours as to which voice we listen to and
follow.

5. Continuance

Continuance is the most important, yet the most difficult of the
Five C's. By now, the prospect has become a convert. The life-changer
must remain close to the convert, to insure that the conversion
experience produces a permanent change:

> Here is where, perhaps, the greatest service can and
> should be performed by the life-changer, and where he or
> she most frequently and regrettably falls down.   The
> convert should receive the most diligent attention in the
> days following his or her conversion.

> It is the testimony of many that just after we have
> taken some step forward in our attempt to live our lives
> on a higher spiritual level, the Tempter is most powerful
> and insidious in its efforts to drag us down.
> (*Soul Surgery*, pp. 132-133, edited)

We must offer support as the convert tests the validity of the
conversion experience:

> It is our responsibility to help the convert to see how
> he or she can remain in the higher attitudes of faith,

resisting the tendency to give way to unworthy moods, and how, when dark times and troubles descend, the convert must persistently stay in the presence of God. Hence the importance of prayer as a daily exercise and a lifelong study. In prayer we breathe the air of faith that defies every temptation, fear and doubt. In prayer our souls become secure in the knowledge that while *we* may fail God, God never fails us. Although we may at times feel no sense of the Divine presence, it does not indicate that God has drawn away from us, but rather we have begun to live by self-will rather than by God's will. (*Soul Surgery*, pp. 134-135, edited)

The convert needs to establish a daily routine of prayer and meditation in order to strengthen faith and resist the "dark forces." We share our guidance with the convert so he or she can see that two-way prayer really works:

The new convert must learn to feed the soul, day by day, on God's living Word revealed in the spiritual literature. Here, too, the convert cannot be left alone, but needs, and will usually welcome, friendly guidance. (*Soul Surgery*, pp. 135-136, edited)

It is essential for the convert to work with others to reinforce and strengthen the conversion experience. We can have a mountain top transformation, but if we do not carry this experience with us in our day-to-day routine of helping others, we will some day start to doubt the authenticity of our change and be drawn back into the darkness:

Here is where we are most prone to failure in this work of continuance. Following conversion, the convert must be set to work to win others. This will be both the test of the reality of the new experience and one of the surest safeguards against it's soon becoming unreal. The

convert should understand from the first that prayer and meditation will ultimately become burdensome, if not actually distasteful, if he or she regards them only as a means for spiritual development, and not also as the fundamental and essential means to successfully serve and win others. The central point around which his or her life now revolves must be serving others.
(*Soul Surgery*, p. 137, edited)

It is our responsibility to make sure the convert is on solid spiritual ground before we turn our attention to someone else:

One excuse we often make for failing to follow up on people, either before or after conversion, is the fact that we have become separated from them. The proverb holds true for us, "Out of sight, out of mind." But here we need to realize the benefits of continued communication. Very often, we can accomplish as much by writing a letter or making a telephone call, as we could through personal contact.
(*Soul Surgery*, pp. 142-143, edited)

This concludes our description of the Five C's of life-changing. We are now ready to put the Five C's to work. The Group provides us with an excellent example of how to do this in a short pamphlet titled *How Do I Begin?* . This piece was written in 1937 by the Rev. Hallen Viney, a chaplain at Downing College, in Cambridge, England.

This is the second pamphlet James Houck mailed me just prior to our first meeting at the Wilson House in East Dorset, VT on March 15, 1996. The first pamphlet, *How to Listen to God*, changed my life. This pamphlet showed me how to change others.

The pamphlet consists of a conversation between a Group

member and someone interested in learning more about a spiritual way of life. I asked James what the Group called these people, thinking there might be a special term used to designate those who were new to the program. James provided an immediate response: "pagans."

The word was quite popular with Group members in the 1930's. Several of the books written during this period even had the word "pagan" in their titles, including *I Was a Pagan* by V. C. Kitchen and *The Eight Points of the Oxford Group–An Exposition for Christians and Pagans* by C. Irving Benson. Even though "pagan" was in general use at the time, I will use the word prospect to denote the person who is interested in learning more about the spiritual way of life practiced by the Group.

The pamphlet opens with the prospect telling the life-changer he is not convinced there is any value to two-way prayer.

Prospect
      "It is all very well for you people to talk, but what I
      want to know is, 'How do you get that way?' There's
      obviously something to this Group business, and what
      I'd like to know is, 'How do I start?' "

The prospect has heard of the Group and knows he is talking to a Group member. The prospect may be skeptical but he is curious nonetheless.

Now it is time for the life-changer to practice the Five C's of Confidence, Confession, Conviction, Conversion and Continuance. Even though this pamphlet was not specifically written to explain this process, the Five C's are clearly illustrated and practiced throughout this conversation.

The life-changer attempts to reply to the question, but the prospect interrupts him. The life-changer is talking about concepts the prospect does not understand. The prospect asks for a simpler explanation—one that he can identify with. It is important for the life-changer to communicate at the prospect's level of understanding.

Life-Changer
> "Well, it's a matter of being in touch with God and----"

Prospect
> "Yes, I know, you all say that, but "touch with God" means nothing to me. What I want to know is, How do I begin? What forms do I fill in? What do I have to do?"

Life-Changer
> "First of all I believe that God wants to talk to you. It is just as simple as that"

The life-changer now has gotten the prospect's attention, but he still has not gotten through the prospect's wall of resistance.

Prospect
> "He's never talked to me."

Life-Changer
> "No, perhaps you have never been within calling distance. It isn't much good saying 'Hello' to a friend if you know beforehand he is looking the other way and not listening. How can God talk to you if you don't listen?"

The life-changer poses a thought-provoking question that allows him to learn more about the prospect. Then the life-changer is given the opportunity to develop the confidence of the prospect.

Prospect
>"But even if I did listen, as you say, God wouldn't talk to me. How could He?"

Life-Changer
>"You haven't tried it yet. Why, people all over the world have tried listening and say that God does talk to them. You need to make the experiment."

So, the life-changer issues the prospect a challenge. Basically, he tells the prospect, "Don't take my word for it, check it out for yourself." He does not try to force some religious philosophy upon the prospect. Rather, he dares the prospect to try it. The prospect rises to the challenge.

Prospect
>"All right, I'll try anything once. What do I do? Shut my eyes or something?"

Now, the life-changer has gained the confidence of the prospect, and is ready to proceed to the next step. The life-changer makes a series of statements about himself to draw the prospect into the Confession phase of the life-changing process.

Life-Changer
>"Remember, there are one or two conditions attached to this listening. It's rather like a telephone–God can't talk through a dirty contact. If you want to hear what He has to say, you must first find out, *as I had to,* whether you've got a good connection."

Prospect

"Well, I probably do have a dirty contact. I don't claim to be a saint, but I am as good as the next man."

Life-Changer

"Exactly, but if you really want to listen to God you have to be more definite. If something goes wrong with the telephone, the repair person doesn't say, 'I know this telephone isn't working very well, but it's as good as the next one.' First of all he or she has got to find the fault in the telephone and correct it. *When I started listening, I had to be just as definite with myself as the repair person was with the telephone.*"

Prospect

"How did you do that?"

Life-Changer

"Well, there are four very good tests that helped me to be definite in finding these faults. They are Honesty, Purity, Unselfishness and Love. *When I first met the Group, I didn't know much about spirituality,* but I *did* know what honesty meant. *When I thought about my life in terms of honesty, some very concrete faults came into my mind. I felt uncomfortable.*"

The life-changer's Confession has drawn the prospect into the conversation. The prospect is more than just curious. He is now genuinely interested in what the life-changer has to say.

Let us review the Confessions the life-changer made during this brief exchange. There were four of them. They are:

1. "If you want to hear what He has to say, you must

first find out, *as I had to*, whether you've got a good connection."

2. *"When I started listening, I had to be just as definite with myself as the repair person was with the telephone."*

3. *"When I first met the Group, I didn't know much about spirituality, but I did know what honesty meant."*

4. *"When I thought about my life in terms of honesty some very concrete faults came into my mind. I felt uncomfortable."*

The life-changer's confessions are:

1. Before I met the Group I also was a nonbelieiver.

2. The Group convinced me I did not have a good connection with God.

3. I looked at my life in terms of the Four Standards of Honesty, Purity, Unselfishness and Love and found I came up short in some areas.

4. I had to be very specific about my shortcomings in order to overcome them.

These disclosures help the prospect to identify with the life-changer. This puts the prospect in a position where he can truthfully say, "Wow, this guy is just like me."

Next, the life-changer strives to instill Conviction in the prospect by taking him through the inventory process. He provides specific instructions on how to discover those aspects of self which have produced a faulty connection with God. The life-changer explains that we get reconnected by writing down and sharing our character liabilities.

Life-Changer

"A good way I found to get reconnected was to take four pieces of paper and head each with one of the Four Standards. Ask yourself the question, 'Where am I not being honest?' Don't say 'everybody does it,' or 'it doesn't matter.' As answers begin to form in your mind don't argue with them, just write them down whatever they are. It's an excellent way to start 'listening-in.' Then go to the next Standard, and so on. I wrote down quite a lot when I started judging my life against the Standards of Honesty, Purity, Unselfishness and Love. In fact, I began to wonder if the paper would hold out."

Prospect

"I can understand that. After I draw up this list, then what do I do?"

Life-Changer

"Well, like the repair person with the faulty telephone, it's not enough just to know what is wrong and leave it at that. You need to make it right. It often means uncomfortable things like apologizing to people and paying back money."

Prospect

"I see what you mean. I begin by writing down everything that is wrong and then I make it right."

Life-Changer

"Yes, that's the first step–as God guides you. But, here is the secret to the entire business. If you make this list honestly, you will find you cannot put things in order yourself. I found, for example, there were habits I knew were wrong which I ought to put right, but every now and then they defeated me. A person can't live up to these Standards on his or her own strength."

Prospect

"How do I do it, if I can't do it by myself?"

Life-Changer

"You need something more than your own strength to deal with your problems. Take fear for instance. You can tell yourself six excellent reasons why you shouldn't be afraid of Mr. So-and-So. You say to yourself over and over that you are *not* afraid of him, and yet you're still afraid. It's the same with worry. You need extra power to get rid of it, don't you?"

Prospect

"Yes, I suppose I do."

Now the life-changer has set the stage for the Conversion experience. He has provided the prospect with a plan of action that will strip away those things which have been blocking him from God.

Life-Changer

"That something more is the power of God. Our Creator provides us with the strength to face all human problems. When we are obedient to what God wants us to do, we are given the power to overcome all difficulties."

Prospect

"I don't know that I follow all that. I'm afraid I don't know much about this spiritual business."

Life-Changer

"Don't worry about the theory now. A lot of people can switch on a light without knowing much about electricity. The main thing is to benefit from the light. In the same way, many people establish and maintain a two-way communication with God without first knowing all the theory. They understand more later, as they gain more experience."

Prospect

"I see. But, how do I get in touch with God?"

Life-Changer

"You have to make up your mind to give God complete control of your life. It is the inward attitude, the surrender of your will, that counts. The question is, do you really mean business? If you do, God will see you through."

Prospect

"I really do want God's help."

The prospect has changed. He realizes he cannot overcome his difficulties by himself and he has invited God into his life. He has been transformed from a prospect to a convert. But, he still has some questions. Here is where the life-changer reinforces the conversion. The life-changer first tells the convert he must listen to God every day and then he provides the convert with guidelines on how to do it.

Life-Changer

"It's a decision for life. It means carrying out God's will seven days a week, twenty-four hours a day."

Convert

"What does that imply in practice?"

Life-Changer

"For one thing it means getting up earlier to listen to God. An alarm clock may help. If you feel chained to your bed, put the clock out of reach across the room."

Convert

"How long should I listen?"

Life-Changer

"As long as you feel you need to. Most of us began with a few minutes and find we need a half hour or so now. Some people sit up in bed with a pencil and notebook. Others dress first."

Convert

"What happens? Do I hear a voice or something?"

Life-Changer

"No, God normally talks to people through their thoughts. It's the natural way for God to reach us. Ask God specific questions about your business, your home life, every bit of the world in which you live. Think over the problems of the day in terms of 'What does God want?' rather than 'What do I want?' We find convictions forming in our mind which show us the right thing to do. We write these convictions down."

Convert

> "Why write them down?"

Life-Changer

> "So we won't forget them. Later, we go over them to see if they've been done."

Convert

> "But how am I to know whether these thoughts are from God?"

Life-Changer

> "You can test them against the Four Standards of Honesty, Purity, Unselfishness and Love. The God thoughts will naturally be in line with what we find in our spiritual literature. If in doubt, you can check them with other people who listen to God."

Here the life-changer has provided the convert with a brief summary of the *How to Listen to God* pamphlet. The life-changer takes the convert through the process and the convert is convinced that two-way prayer will work in his life. The convert has a psychic change which produces a new perception of God and the world around him. The life-changer has provided the convert with the answer to all of his difficulties.

Convert

> "Yes, that sounds practical enough. I need to talk all of it over with someone who has already taken the plunge so I can see things really straight. Most of us, you know, are experts at deceiving ourselves. As I understand it, first of all I have to be honest with myself and then take my orders from God every day."

Life-Changer
  "Yes, that is the purpose of the Group, to put God in control of people like you and me.

  "Selfish, self-centeredness is the real problem. Change that and we are well on our way to solving social, economic, and political problems. Everyone admits moral recovery has to come before economic recovery can be permanent. Besides, God-controlled people make God-controlled nations, and God-controlled nations can achieve world peace."

Then, the life-changer ends the conversation by issuing a challenge to us all.

Life-Changer
  "That's why I am part of this life-changing movement. I'm putting all I have into it. Why don't *you* give it a try?"

This program of life-changing based on the Five C's of Confidence, Confession, Conviction, Conversion and Continuance has produced countless miracles over the years. All you have to do is listen to God, follow guidance and use this simple outline to help those who are still living in the darkness.

Who knows, you may just change a life or two along the way. That is what this spiritual journey is all about: "Changing the world–one life at a time."

12

The Journey Continues

During the summer of 1999, I took a six-week trip from the East Coast through the Midwest to visit some of the Guidance Meetings and Groups that had recently formed as the direct result of the distribution of the *How to Listen to God* pamphlet. I had just been laid off as a water treatment consultant to some of the Arizona Copper mines, and I needed a break from the corporate world to whom I had dedicated the past thirty years of my life.

I conducted the trip based on "faith and prayer," which entailed living without income or self-support This is how many of the Oxford Group teams operated in the 1930's.

From Fryeburg, Maine to Chicago, Illinois, people took me in and helped with my expenses. I attended their local meetings and did what I could to help bring people closer to God. I was richly blessed with an abundance of heartfelt love and sincere comradery at each stop on my spiritual odyssey.

I spent a week in Timonium, Maryland, with James Houck, who lives with his daughter and son-in-law, Bet-C and Bud Sammis. They reside in separate houses on a two and one half lot about twelve miles north of downtown Baltimore.

James is responsible for the upkeep and maintenance of the grounds which he does with the help of a tractor lawn mower. He showed me a family scrapbook detailing his exploits as "Bradshaw, the groundskeeper."

It was hilarious viewing a series of photographs depicting James weeding one of the large flower beds. He numbered the rocks as he removed them from among the flowers. After he finished the weeding, he put the rocks back based on his numbering sequence.

I had brought my digital video camera to record some of James' life-changing accomplishments in the Baltimore area. In addition to the hundred thousand lives he has touched in the recovery community, he has also made a significant impact on the children of the Baltimore school system and the longshoremen on the Baltimore waterfront.

Yes, James Houck truly is a remarkable man. Over the years he has helped so many, and, even in his mid-nineties, he is continuing to do so. He claims no special talent in the area of life-changing. He just listens to God and follows guidance.

I interviewed the principal and counselor at the Sparks Elementary school, where James had implemented an ethics program a few years before. This was a revolutionary grass-roots program that had changed the lives of thousands of children by teaching them to judge everything they thought, said and did based upon a set of standards. It was obvious from the enthusiastic response I received from Tom Ellis and Laura Hudson, that James had changed their lives also.

Tom and Laura spent two hours describing the positive contribution James Houck has made, not only to the Sparks

Elementary School, but to the entire Baltimore school system. As the direct result of the success at Sparks school, the program has been implemented in six schools from kindergarten through the twelfth grade. Tom read a memo from the superintendent of the Baltimore school system suggesting that all schools consider implementing James' program.

James' life-changing efforts had been detailed in a newspaper article that highlighted the points covered during the videotaped interview:

Volunteer, 92-Years-Old, Brings Ethics Program to Life at Sparks School

North County News   January 22, 1998
by Lavinia Edmunds

At 92, Jim Houck is still thinking of new ways to change the world. The ethics program he developed for students at Sparks Elementary School, with the help of guidance counselor Laura Hudson, has become something of a mission for the nonagenarian.

"They call me Mr. Four-Ways," says Houck, looking dapper in his dark gray suit and paisley tie on a recent day at the Sparks school. The nickname, the Timonium resident explains, refers to the Four-Way Test used by the Rotary Clubs nationwide. The test consists of four questions an individual is supposed to ask of every action: Is it the TRUTH? –Is it FAIR to all concerned? –Will it build GOOD WILL and better friendships? –and Will it be

BENEFICIAL to all concerned? Now students at Sparks recite these questions instead of the Pledge of Allegiance every school day.

The way the program works, Houck explains, is that students are "caught" doing good acts during the school day, from sharing crayons to turning in food money. Names are put into a box in each classroom and on the last Thursday of the month, known as Four-Way Day, one name is drawn from each box for prizes, including pizza and T-shirts.

Sparks students say the program has made a difference. Ten-year-old Maria Jensen, a Four-Way winner, says Sparks students seem to fight less than students at neighboring schools and are more focused on looking for the good in others. "When you do right, other people want to do things right and it keeps going," Jensen explains.

In his forty-nine years with local Rotary Clubs–first in Towson and now with Hunt Club–Houck has distributed book covers, devised a coloring contest for kindergartners, and promoted an essay contest for high schools–all relating to the principles of the Four-Way Test.

Three years ago, when he delivered a flier for a poster contest to Sparks Elementary School, he discussed with principal Tom Ellis the idea of starting a full-blown ethics program. "A lot of times we say to kids 'be good,' but we don't say what 'be good' is," says Ellis, who encouraged Houck to work with the school's guidance counselor, Laura

Hudson.

All Baltimore County schools are encouraged to have 'values' programs, according to school spokesman Donald Mohler, but due to the cultural diversity of the county's students, religious systems cannot be used. With the Four-Way Test, Houck explains, "You can be moral without being religious."

A religious man himself, as a longtime member of Towson United Methodist Church Houck says the principle of honesty, which is central to the Four-Way Test, turned his life around. In 1918, when he was 12 years old, and making $3 a week at an electrical store, Houck recalled stealing supplies to wire his own home. "We were dirt poor–didn't have any electricity," he explained. Sixteen years later, he served on a church committee with the man who had been the head of the electrical store. He sought him out, told him of his crime and paid the money back.

The reaction of the man from whom he stole was a source of unexpected gratification. "He told me no one had ever been so honest with him," Houck said. "Then he confessed that he had been going out on his wife, and that he and his wife were on the brink of signing divorce papers."

Houck said his confession prompted the man to be honest with his wife and try for a reconciliation. "Then I could see the meaning of restitution, of putting things right that are wrong. It does something for everyone," says Houck.

The following day, James took me down to the Baltimore docks. It did not take long to realize just how dangerous it was there. And yet, here was a man who received guidance in 1971 to clean up the port of Baltimore and, not only did he follow through on what he heard, but he lived through the experience.

People do not just visit the port of Baltimore. Those who are not longshoremen are looked upon with great suspicion, especially since considerable illegal activity regularly takes place there. James could have been mistaken for an informant or spy at any time.

As some of the people we met explained, they just could not figure James out. Nobody had ever gone on the docks without an ulterior motive. Certainly no one had ever tried to change lives in such an environment by teaching the principles of two-way prayer.

We first met with Horace Alston, vice president of the International Longshoremen's Association. He is in charge of all union activities at the port of Baltimore. All local ILA union presidents report to him.

Horace said he had known James since the 1970's and that James had played an integral part in bringing two local unions together during a particularly difficult time. One union was 90% black and the other 90% white. The Federal government was forcing them to integrate into one union. There was nothing but strife, threats, and occasional violence between the two warring factions. James stepped right into the middle of the fray and brought the two sides together.

Horace said it was James who showed him how to listen to and follow guidance. He relayed a story about receiving guidance to write a letter that resulted in his elevation from recording secretary of a local union to vice president of the ILA in charge of the Baltimore port. This miraculous transition took place in a matter of weeks. He quickly became a believer in the value of listening to God.

Next, we had lunch followed by a tour of the docks with Bill Schonowski, one of the local union presidents who also had his life changed by James Houck. Bill experienced a spiritual transformation while in prison that put him on a different path. Then, James taught him to follow guidance, which gave Bill the strength and direction to become a very effective life-changer on the Baltimore docks.

In the 1970's, Bill was president of one of the two warring unions at the port of Baltimore. In 1975, he was convicted of illegally accepting money to suspend some union rules. He served eleven months at the Allenwood federal prison.

While incarcerated, Bill met Charles Colson, the former assistant to President Nixon who was serving a prison term for obstruction of justice during Watergate. Charles had started a prison ministry and Bill attended one of his religious assemblies. There, Bill surrendered his life to God

In the years following his release, Bill worked with James to reconcile the racial conflict between the unions. They converted the barriers of prejudice and mistrust into bridges of mutual respect and cooperation.

Next James took me to the home of Dewey Parrish, one of the black union members. He told me he had never eaten at a white man's table before James had invited him to dinner. On numerous occasions, James had brought members of both unions home to discuss their differences in an atmosphere of love and understanding.   Many members of both unions learned the value of two-way prayer and guidance around the Houck dining room table.

James' work on the docks was written up in a newsletter titled Breakthroughs:

Life in the Guided Lane
Breakthroughs Newsletter: 1989

In his lapel, retired Baltimore businessman Jim Houck carries the twin flags of the USA and ILA, the International Longshoremen's Association. He also wears the wheel of the Rotary International, which he supports enthusiastically. Jim retired after twenty years as a manufacturer's representative in 1966, and in 1971 he found a new calling which he has pursued steadfastly since.

He was at a conference in Trois Rivieres (Three Rivers), Canada in 1971, when he had a surprising thought during a "quiet time" to "take on the port of Baltimore." This was surprising to Jim, because during his long years in business he had nothing to do with labor. In fact, he had often disagreed with their ideals and practices. And he knew nothing of the Baltimore docks! But he decided to go.

Jim did not know where to start, but he remembered that port workers in Rio de Janeiro had made a feature film of their experiences (with two-way prayer) titled "Men of Brazil," and he thought this might give him an entree. When he had the opportunity to invite one of the Rio dock workers to Baltimore, he did so, and arranged a meeting between him, several local shippers and the head of the ILA. This opened the door, and the film was shown five times in the port over the years. An ex-convict, who had found a new purpose for his life through the Charles Colson Prison Fellowship, was eager to see Jim's ideas spread and he introduced Jim to many of the rank and file. Often Jim dropped by the headquarters of one of the locals or went down to the port for lunch. At times he was at the port four or five days a week

At first people on the docks couldn't figure Jim out. As one man said, "No one goes to the port who doesn't want something." Jim did want something. His concern was that, in times of crisis, both labor and management searched for "Who's right, rather than what's right." James was interested in changing this philosophy which earned him the nickname of Mister "What's Right." To back his message, he had a thousand pens made with the slogan "What is right, rather than who is right" on them, which he gave away. As a result of the trust he has established, he often gets calls for his thoughts when negotiations are in progress, or when there is trouble on the docks.

As Jim sought God's direction on how to proceed in the ports, he grew in his appreciation of the need for teamwork. The issue dividing the dock workers was race. The two principal union locals, with roughly 2,500 members each, were divided among racial lines. Despite laws decreeing integration, one remained 90% white and the other 90% black. Jim and his wife Betty, who died last year (1988) after 58 years of marriage, entertained many of the longshoremen in their home. One black man, who had found fellowship with white Christians impossible, said at the Houck's, "I just want to say I feel perfectly at home here. It is the first time I have ever sat at a white man's table." The presence of many longshoremen at Betty's funeral spoke volumes.

Jim was particularly gratified by a recent event. A hospital in Nigeria was in urgent need of medical equipment. Through Jim's efforts a local medical center donated $200,000 worth of beds, EKG units, incubators, and other equipment. Through the ex-convict's efforts, the shipping companies agreed to transport the donated items at no charge, and the longshoremen offered to load the medical equipment for nothing. Horace Alston, International Vice-President of the ILA, personally helped load the containers with equipment, as did the president and the treasurer of the local union. For Jim, the effort was a demonstration of Baltimore as it should be, "black and white, management and labor, working spontaneously together without any reward, giving something to help someone else."

Early one evening, I asked Bet-C if I could interview her for the *How to Listen to God* book. Being an unpretentious lady in her sixties, it took some coaxing to get her to agree to be videotaped. I explained the importance of recording her recollections about "quiet time and guidance" as a child. Since James was such an avid proponent of two-way prayer, I wanted to know how he practiced these principles in his family affairs.

I led Bet-C to the back porch. The area was perfect for a video shoot: brightly lit and quiet, except for a few birds chirping in the background.

After a couple of light and sound checks, I asked Bet-C if she was ready. With the Canon XL-1 on my shoulder, I started recording. I almost turned the camera off after Bet-C answered my first question. I am grateful I didn't because she provided me with one of the best pieces of spiritual insight I have ever recorded.

I opened the interview with a little background information:

Wally
"This interview is being conducted on August 2, 1999. I am at the home of Bet-C and Bud Sammis, the daughter and son-in-law of James Houck.

"James Houck has been practicing 'quiet time and guidance' for more than sixty years. This afternoon I hope we can get a little different perspective on his life-changing efforts from one of his children. Bet-C, thank you for providing me this opportunity to learn more about your father and how he practiced the Oxford Group program while you were growing up."

Bet-C
"Glad to do it,"

Wally
    "Bet-C, can you tell me how practicing 'quiet time and guidance' has changed your life?"

Bet-C
    "It hasn't changed my life at all.

    Wally, let me explain. 'Quiet time and guidance' hasn't changed my life–it is the only life I've ever known. I have nothing to compare it to.

    "Even when I was too little to write, I remember our 'quiet time.' Before breakfast, we would get quiet and listen. During breakfast we would share. Mom, Dad and my two older brothers would share what they had written, I would share what I had heard. I wanted to learn how to write so I could do it the same way they did.

    "Throughout my childhood, 'quiet time' was part of our daily routine. When I was in highschool, I started to question what we were doing. The other kids at school weren't listening to God and I didn't want to be different.

    "After awhile I even started to resent my parents because of the 'quiet time.' I looked forward to leaving home so I wouldn't have to do it anymore.

    "When I left for college, I stopped practicing 'quiet time.' I remember being elated at first, but after a couple of weeks I started feeling confused, and out of sorts. That's when I went back to 'quiet time' and back to writing guidance.

    "I'm not saying I have followed guidance all the time. I've had my share of difficulties. But, each time I get into trouble, I know why. It's because I've been trying to do something by myself without God's help.

"So, you see, I've been trying to follow guidance all my life. I've never known what it's like not to have God in charge."

I am not sure how many other Bet-C's there are out there, but I do know that, because of the *How to Listen to God* pamphlet, there is a new generation of children being raised on two-way prayer.

I have received numerous telephone calls from men and women who are not only practicing "quiet time and guidance" with their spouses but also with their children. Yes, the *How to Listen to God* pamphlet is changing the world, one life at a time and one family at a time.

Since that visit in the summer of 1999, I have watched James' popularity soar. The crowds at the spiritual conferences and workshops have kept getting larger and larger. Additional newspaper and magazine articles have honored him for his many contributions.

In April of this year, James received a prestigious honor from the Rotary club. The details of this award were described in the Towson Times, one of Baltimore suburban newspapers:

Rotarians Honor Member for Inspiration He Lends
The Towson Times   April 12, 2000
by Seanna Kelly Coffin

Upper: Certificate of recognition issued by the Baltimore Board of Education to James Houck for his outstanding contribution to the Baltimore County Public Schools (November 1997)

Lower: James and Wally at a Rotary meeting at the Hunt Valley Group outside of Baltimore, Maryland (August 1999)

James Houck Sr. is not fascinating simply because he's 94.

A charismatic character who defies all the tired assumptions of someone who is nearing the century mark, Houck is lively, passionate and driven. And the Timonium, MD resident believes he still has much to do to help people live loving and fulfilling lives. Consequently, he can often be found behind the wheel of a car or seated on an airplane, on his way to speak at conferences around the country.

That calling has been his mantra since December 12, 1934, when he joined the Oxford Group–an organization that was the foundation for the Twelve Step Movement. "The originator of the Oxford Group was interested in bringing change," said Houck, a friendly and funny man who admits he began drinking alcohol at age five. "He had a program to change the world. But you had to change yourself first. You can't give away something you never had. He wanted you to apply yourself to help meet someone else's need." And that's what Jim has been doing since that momentous weekend at the Frederick, MD, YMCA during the height of the Great Depression. He still remains committed to the ideals and values of the Oxford Group. Over the years, Jim has broadened his horizons and has been of service as a Rotary member for the last 52 years.

The service projects he has championed as a member of the Towson chapter and currently with the Hunt Valley group earned him the coveted

"Rotary Service Above Self" award last month. He was one of only 150 Rotarians worldwide to be cited. According to Nigel House, president of the Hunt Valley chapter who nominated Jim for the award, there are 1.2 million members in 29,000 clubs around the world.

His favorite role as a Rotarian has been introducing the Four-Way Test to students. The test asks students to contemplate Four Standards similar to the Oxford edicts of Honesty, Purity, Unselfishness and Love. They are: Is it the truth? Is it fair to all concerned? Will it build good will and better friendships? Will it be beneficial to all concerned?

Participants are asked to answer the questions in different ways. Kindergartners compete in a coloring contest, elementary school students are required to draw posters, middle school students write essays and high school students give speeches. Everyone who attempts the task is rewarded and prizes are given for the best work at each grade level.

Jim's leadership in the Four-Way Test is a hint of all that he has pursued as a Rotarian. House recalled a recent cool morning when chapter members were asked to go to the McCormick Road to clean up litter in coordination with the "Adopt-a-Road Program." One of the first people to arrive was Jim. "The man is a living example of how you should live you life and how to help the community," House said. "He is really totally committed. You just don't realize how many people he has helped along the way."

Jim is a sought after speaker at seminars for people in recovery. He said he aims to help his peers do more than just remain sober–he wants to encourage them to give to others as he has learned to do.

For the next few months, he has speaking engagements scheduled around the country. "You have to give as much of yourself as you can to meet the need of others," he said. "For me, this was the life-changing formula: You have to gain someone's confidence, offer your confession which brings conviction, witness the person's conversion, and then continue to help that person to change others."

I have been absolutely blessed to have traveled and observed James Houck in action for the past four years. As Ronnie said when introducing James in Dayton, Ohio in November 1997, "I am so excited to be in the midst of something this awesome–something that will happen only once in my lifetime."

Before I close this labor of love, this testimonial to a man who has meant so much to so many, I want to take a moment to address one more subject: the Big Voice. Until this point, I have been describing how God speaks to us via the "still small voice." We pray to God through our thoughts and God answers our prayers and petitions through our thoughts. But, in addition to this Small Voice which all of us can hear anytime we're willing to listen, there is another voice–the Big Voice–which some of us hear from time to time. In my case, the Voice has been so loud and definitive, I've been able to remember verbatim what was said on each occasion.

In the late 1970's, I heard the Big Voice three times. The first time, the Voice proved to me it was the Voice of God. The second time, the Voice saved my life and the third time, the voice directed me to save the lives of two others.

The first time I heard the Big Voice was about eight 'o clock on a week night as I was driving home from work. At the time, I was consulting for several of the oil refineries in the Puget Sound area of western Washington. It was midwinter, and raining as it usually does that time of the year.

I was traveling south along the highway toward Seattle. I was about forty miles north of the city when I heard the 'Voice.' I was so shocked, I pulled the car over to the side of the road to look for someone in the back seat. When I realized I was alone, I thought about what I had heard. The Voice said, "Drive to Gold Bar and buy some fence posts."

This was an unusual request. Gold Bar was a very small logging town over an hour's drive to the east. By the time I arrived, there certainly would be no store open where I could buy fence posts.

At the time, I was building a cabin about twenty miles east of Gold Bar. I had to drive through Gold Bar each time I went to the cabin. Yes, there was a place in town that sold fence posts. But, I was not in the market for fence posts, especially in the middle of a rainy, midwinter night.

But, the Voice was so loud and its directions so clear, I turned off the highway and headed to Gold Bar. At nine thirty

I pulled up in front of the lot where the fence posts were for sale. Sure enough, the lot was closed. That is when I noticed for the first time that there was a mobile home behind the lot. The light next to the front door was on.

I drove along a dirt road to the mobile home. I went up to the door and knocked. Almost immediately, a woman opened the door.

Not knowing how to explain why I was there, I blurted out, "I'm here to buy some fence posts." She smiled and replied, "I know, God told me you were coming."

She invited me in. She read something from an open bible which was next to her chair in front of the fireplace. We talked for about an hour. She then said a prayer for me, asking God to relieve my burdens and protect me during my spiritual journey. I thanked her and left.

In the next nine months I spent a considerable amount of time with this woman and her husband. It was as if I had been placed in a position of neutrality, safe and secure.

During this time, I heard the Big Voice two more times. On the slopes of Mount Baker, the Voice said, "Kick off your skis." I grabbed a tree branch to steady myself so I could comply with the request and found myself at the edge of a 200-foot cliff. If I had not listened to the Voice, I would have gone over the cliff and been killed upon impact.

Returning from a business trip in eastern Washington, I was driving through a mountain pass during the first snow of the season. When I reached the turnoff for a road that was closed for the winter, the Voice said, "Take the road to the right." I took the closed road, worked my way through several inches of snow for ten miles, and rescued two people who were stranded and about to freeze to death.

But then I fell back into the darkness of addiction. I returned to worshiping the false gods of money and power. I continued to be successful in my career but I became more and more detached from the Voice. I did not hear the Big Voice again for fourteen years.

In 1988, I found a new way of living. Four years later, I heard the Big Voice for the fourth time. It was at the Wilson House in East Dorset, Vermont, where I was to meet James four years later. This time the Voice said, "You're not here to buy a Big Book."

What I learned on this occasion was the value of sharing guidance with another person. I thought the Voice said not to buy the book I had traveled three thousand miles to acquire. The book seller thought the Voice was trying to tell me I was at the Wilson House for some other purpose.

He was right. The next day, I was able to prevent a woman from committing suicide by sharing my guidance with her.

The fifth time I heard the Big Voice was December 1999. I was walking a piece of vacant land I owned in Tucson, AZ. The Voice said, "Sell the land, I'll provide you with a church." I immediately called James to tell him what I had heard.

James listened attentively and then asked what I thought the guidance meant. I told him it appeared to me that I was being called into the ministry. Maybe it was time to enroll in a divinity school. James said he would have to pray on this one;

as far as he was concerned, I was already doing God's work. He had seen many lives changed as the result of the *Back to Basics* and the *Converting Barriers to Bridges* programs.

James shared his thoughts with me in the form of a letter written on January 7, 2000. He believed my guidance was from God, but he questioned my interpretation of it.

He wrote:

> "It was nice talking to you the other evening. I had definite guidance to call you. It was strange how definite it was. But, after talking to you, I understand why."

> "Wally, I have very definite feeling there are changes going on–that your philosophy of life is changing. Sometimes we get the feeling we want to change things and apply what we believe to be God's will in different ways.

> "Just the other night, in our phone conversation, you mentioned again our first time at the Wilson House and how you learned to listen to God. God has brought you a long way since that time, and is using your life in a whole new and wonderful way. I don't think you can question this. You have brought a vast number of people to God. My concern is that what you are considering now will minimize your effectiveness in the future.

> "There is no question that God has laid His Hands on you. He has big plans for you, but I don't believe they will be accomplished with your new

thinking. I feel you are pulling in your horns. You are losing your world vision.

"You mentioned 'a church'–that your guidance was to have a church. This would gravely reduce your activity. Churches have a limited outreach. I know you will say it depends on what goes on in the church. But a church minimizes the number we can reach with our message. With the misdirected millions, we have 'worlds to conquer.' These are the unsheparded masses we started out to contact, and I think this is the route God wants us to take. But, we cannot move without you. You are God's chosen leader for this work. You already have a church. It is the streets, half way houses and treatment centers of the world–anywhere people are reaching out for help.

"You may say I am way off base, but Wally, I have been around this life-changing business a long time, and I generally can tell when it "looks like rain." Stay in the sunshine and continue doing what you are doing.

"Think about it and get back to me. Let's talk about it. I love you and want you to be the person God wants you to be.

As ever,

Jim"

At first I was a little surprised by the tone and substance of the letter, but after I thought about it for a while, I realized he was right. Millions need to learn how to listen to God. I would be significantly reducing my ability to help people, if I spent the rest of my life concentrating on a small congregation in a corner of Tucson, Arizona.

After praying and meditating on James' letter, I realized the significance of what he had to say. Wow! I already have a church. It is a grass roots ministry, with services held in living rooms, church basements and recovery centers.

All of us need to consider practicing the teachings of James Houck. There is much work to be done. The world can be a better place if each of us is willing to do our part.

Several years ago, James provided me with a Group meditation book titled *A New Day*. In it I found a passage written by a French theologian more than one hundred years ago. This short essay clearly states that each of us can make a difference. The choice is ours. We can change the world:

> The world that you want to transform in a just manner will not be transformed because you yourselves are not transformed. And so long as you refuse to change yourselves, the world will not change. But the world can change if you change.

> How do you change? By listening to God; because, as the sun is always shining, so God is constantly speaking. (When) do you listen to God? The best time is in the morning, before all distractions and activities intervene. How can you listen to God, you ask? This is the answer—you write. Write, so that you may better hear the Word that is in you and better keep His instructions.

Auguste Gratry, 1805-72

When we have a "quiet time" each morning, we start the day by renewing our faith in God. We listen to the Voice within so we will always know God's plan for us.

We pause when agitated so we can get reconnected to the source of all Power. When negative or self-destructive thoughts enter our minds, we acknowledge and identify them for what they are–thoughts based in self rather than thoughts from God. "We have ceased fighting anything," even our thoughts. We do not try to control our thoughts or try to make them go away. Just by acknowledging them, they go away on their own.

We discuss our thoughts with another who is also listening to God. "More light comes in through two windows than one." Then, God will fill our minds with all that is harmonious, beautiful, and enduring.

In the evening, we review our guidance to determine how closely we followed God's plan for us. Upon completing this review, we ask God to forgive us for our shortcomings and ask for His continued guidance and support in our future activities.

Walk all the way with God. Make God a good companion by praying often. Do not let your contact with God be broken. Step out in faith as you travel the path of life. Know that you are safe and protected wherever God leads you. "Keep on the firing line of life with these motives and God will keep you unharmed."

Yes, there is a war going on, but unlike Vietnam, this is a war we can win. The plan of action is simple: get quiet, listen, record what you hear, check with others and obey. Judge everything you think, say or do based on Honesty, Purity, Unselfishness and Love. It is a time-tested plan that can not fail.

In all of us there is an inner consciousness that is the "God who speaks." It is an intimate and personal Voice that reveals itself in time of quiet meditation. "It is like a lamp unto our feet and a light unto our path."

We can dispel the darkness by allowing God's radiant presence to gently guide us. And with God's quiet whisper leading the way, our Creator will show us new horizons and lead us to places we have never been before. "This is an experience you must not miss."

"The bridge to the future can only be built upon the stepping stones of the past."
> Wally Paton
> Guidance, Sept. 18, 1999
> Mackinac Island, MI

Appendices

Bibliography

How to Listen to God pamphlet

Bibliography

Batterson, John. *How to Listen to God.* unpublished, n.d.

Benson, C. Irving. *The Eight Points of the Oxford Group.* Melborne: Oxford University Press, 1936

Blair, Emily Newell. *"The Oxford Group Challenges America".* New York: Hearst Magazines Inc.,(Good Housekeeping), October 1936

Clark, Walter H. *The Oxford Group-Its History and Significance.* New York: Bookman Associates, 1951

Forde, Eleanor Napier, *The Guidance of God.* Oxford: Oxford University, 1927

Jones, E. Stanley. *Victorious Living.* New York: Abington–Cokesbury Press, 1936

Kitchen, Victor C. *I Was a Pagan.* New York: Harper & Brothers, 1934

Rose, Cecil. *When Man Listens.* New York: Oxford University Press, 1937

Russell, Arthur J. *For Sinners Only.* London: Hodder & Stoughton, 1932

Sangster, W. E. *God Does Guide Us*. New York: The Abingdon Press, 1934

Streeter, Burnett Hillman *The God Who Speaks*. New York: the Macmillan Company, 1936

The Layman with a Notebook. *What is the Oxford Group?* London: Oxford University Press, 1933

Thornton-Duesbury, Julian P. *Sharing*, The Oxford Group, n.d.

Viney, Hallen, *How Do I Begin?* Camden, NJ: The Haddon Craftsman, Inc., 1937

Walter, Howard A. *Soul Surgery*. Calcutta: Association Press (Y.M.C.A. of India and Ceylon), 1919

HOW TO LISTEN TO GOD

These are a few simple suggestions for people who are willing to make an experiment. You can discover for yourself the most important and practical thing any human being can ever learn—how to be in touch with God.

All that is needed is the ***willingness to try it honestly***. Every person who has done this consistently and sincerely has found that it really works.

Before you begin, look over these fundamental points. They are true and are based on the experience of thousands of people.

1. God is alive. He always has been and He always will be.

2. God knows everything.

3. God can do anything.

4. God can be everywhere–all at the same time. (These are the important differences between God and us human beings.)

5. God is invisible–we can't see Him or touch Him–but ***God is here***. He is with you now. He is beside you. He surrounds you. He fills the room or the whole place where you are right now. He is in you now. He is in your heart.

6. God cares very much for ***you***. He is interested in you. He has a plan for your life. He has an answer for every need and problem you face.

7. God will tell you all that you ***need*** to know. He will not always tell you all that you ***want*** to know.

8. God will help you do anything that He asks you to do.

9. Anyone can be in touch with God, anywhere and at any time, ***if the conditions are obeyed.***

   These are the conditions:

   - To be quiet and still
   - To listen
   - To be honest about every thought that comes
   - To test the thoughts to be sure that they come from God
   - To obey

So, with these basic elements as a background, here are specific suggestions on how to listen to God:

1. *Take Time*
Find some place and time where you can be alone, quiet and undisturbed. Most people have found that the early morning is the best time. Have with you some paper and pen or pencil.

2. *Relax*
Sit in a comfortable position. Consciously relax all your muscles. Be loose. There is no hurry. There needs to be no strain during these minutes. God cannot get through to us if we are tense and anxious about later responsibilities.

3. *Tune In*
Open your heart to God. Either silently or aloud, just say to God in a natural way that you would like to find His plan for your life—you want His answer to the problem or situation that you are facing just now. Be definite and specific in your request.

4. *Listen*
Just be still, quiet, relaxed and open. Let your mind go "loose." Let God do the talking. Thoughts, ideas, and impressions will begin to come into your mind and heart. Be alert and aware and open to every one.

5. *Write!*
Here is the important key to the whole process. Write down everything that comes into your mind. *Everything*. Writing is simply a means of recording so that you can remember later. ***Don't*** sort out or edit your thoughts at this point.

Don't say to yourself:
> This thought isn't important;
> This is just an ordinary thought;
> This can't be guidance;
> This isn't nice;
> This can't be from God;
> This is just me thinking, etc.

Write down everything that passes through your mind:
> Names of people;
> Things to do;
> Things to say;
> Things that are wrong and need to be made right.

Write down everything:
> Good thoughts–bad thoughts;
> Comfortable thoughts–uncomfortable thoughts;
> "Holy" thoughts–"unholy" thoughts;
> Sensible thoughts–"crazy" thoughts.

Be Honest! Write down ***everything***. A thought comes quickly, and it escapes even more quickly unless it is captured and put down.

6. *Test*
When the flow of thoughts slows down, stop. Take a good look at what you have written. ***Not every thought we have comes from God.*** So we need to test our thoughts. Here is where the written record helps us to be able to look at them.
a) Are these thoughts completely ***honest, pure, unselfish and loving?***
b) Are these thoughts in line with our duties to our family, to our country?
c) Are these thoughts in line with our understanding of the teachings found in our spiritual literature?

7. *Check*
When in doubt and when it is important, what does another person who is living two-way prayer think about this thought or action? More light comes in through two windows than one. Someone else who also wants God's plan for our lives may help us to see more clearly.

Talk over together what you have written. Many people do this. They tell each other what guidance has come. This is the secret of unity. There are always three sides to every question—your side, my side, and the right side. Guidance shows us which is the right side—not who is right, but what is right.

8. *Obey*
Carry out the thoughts that have come. You will only be sure of guidance as you go through with it. A rudder will not guide a boat until the boat is moving. As you obey, very often the results will convince you that you are on the right track.

9. *Blocks?*
What if I don't seem to get any definite thoughts? God's guidance is as freely available as the air we breathe. If I am not receiving thoughts when I listen the fault is not Gods.

Usually it is because there is something ***I will not do:***
> something wrong in my life that I will not face and make right;

a habit or indulgence I will not give up;
a person I will not forgive;
a wrong relationship in my life I will not give up;
a restitution I will not make;
something God has already told me to do that I will not obey.

Check these points and be honest. Then try listening again.

10. *Mistakes*
Suppose I make a mistake and do something in the name of God that isn't right? Of course we make mistakes. We are humans with many faults. However, ***God will always honor our sincerity.***

He will work around and through every honest mistake we make. He will help us make it right. ***But remember this!*** sometimes when we do obey God, someone else may not like it or agree with it. So when there is opposition, it doesn't always mean you have made a mistake. It can mean that the other person doesn't want to know or to do what is right.

Suppose I fail to do something that I have been told and the opportunity to do it passes? There is only one thing to do. Put it right with God. Tell Him you're sorry. Ask Him to forgive you, then accept His forgiveness and begin again. God is our Father—He is not an impersonal calculator. He understand us far better than we do.

11. *Results*
We never know what swimming is like until we get down into the water and try. We will never know what this is like until we sincerely try it.

Every person who has tried this honestly finds that a wisdom, not their own, comes into their minds and that Power greater than human power begins to operate in their lives. It is an endless adventure.

There is a way of life, for everyone, everywhere. Anyone can be in touch with the living God, anywhere, anytime, ***if we fulfill His conditions:***

> ***When man listens, God Speaks.***
> ***When man obeys, God Acts.***

This is the law of prayer.

God's plan for this world goes forward through the lives of ordinary people who are willing to be governed by Him.

John E. Batterson